**Volume 15, Issue 2** June 2011

# New European Fashion Centers: Dreams of Small Nations in a Polycentric Fashion World

Special Issue
Edited by Lise Skov and Marie Riegels Melchior

Fashion Theory
The Journal of Dress, Body & Culture

## Aims and Scope

**The importance of studying the body as a site for the deployment of discourses is well-established in a number of disciplines. By contrast, the study of fashion has, until recently, suffered from a lack of critical analysis. Increasingly, however, scholars have recognized the cultural significance of self-fashioning, including not only clothing but also such body alterations as tattooing and piercing. *Fashion Theory* takes as its starting point a definition of "fashion" as the cultural construction of the embodied identity. It provides an interdisciplinary forum for the rigorous analysis of cultural phenomena ranging from footbinding to fashion advertising.**

Anyone wishing to submit an article, interview, or a book, film or exhibition review for possible publication in this journal should contact Valerie Steele (at the address listed to the right) or the Editorial Department at Berg Publishers, 1st Floor, Angel Court, 81 St Clements Street, Oxford, OX4 1AW, UK; e-mail: icritchley@bergpublishers.com.

Please send all books for review to the Book Reviews Editor



Berg Publishers is the imprint of Bloomsbury Publishing Plc.



ISSN (print): 1362-704X
ISSN (online): 1751-7419

www.bergpublishers.com

## Ordering Information

Four issues per volume. One volume per annum. 2011: Volume 15

**By mail:**
Customer Services
Turpin Distribution
Stratton Business Park
Pegasus Drive
Biggleswade
SG18 8TQ
UK

**By fax:** +44 (0) 1767 601640
**By telephone:** +44 (0) 1767 604951
**By e-mail:** custserv@turpin-distribution.com

## Subscription Rates

**Institutional (print and online):** (1 year) £313, US$611; (2 year) £501, US$977
**Institutional (online only):** (1 year) £266, US$519; (2 year) £426, US$831
**Individuals (print only):** (1 year) £49, US$85; (2 year) £78, US$136
Institutional subscriptions include two issues of *Fashion Practice*.

Full color images available online.
Access your electronic subscription through www.ingentaconnect.com

## Inquiries

Editorial and Production: Ian Critchley, Managing Editor,
e-mail: icritchley@bergpublishers.com
Advertising and subscriptions: Ellie Graves,
e-mail: egraves@bergpublishers.com

## Reprints of Individual Articles

Copies of individual articles may be obtained from the Publishers at the appropriate fees.
Write to:
Berg Publishers,
1st Floor, Angel Court,
81 St Clements Street,
Oxford,
OX4 1AW,
UK.

Printed in the United Kingdom.

JUNE 2011

*Fashion Theory* is indexed by the following abstracting/indexing services: Abstracts in Anthropology; AIO Anthropological Index Online; ARTbibliographies Modern; British Humanities Index; Current Contents/Arts & Humanities; DAAI Design and Applied Arts Index; IBR International Bibliography of Book Reviews of Scholarly Literature in the Humanities and Social Sciences; IBSS International Bibliography of the Social Sciences; IBZ International Bibliography of Periodical Literature on the Humanities and Social Sciences; ISI Arts and Humanities Citation Index; Scopus; Sociological Abstracts

Page 137

Page 157

Page 177

Page 201

Page 225

Page 239

# Contents

*Fashion Theory,* Volume 15, Issue 2, pp. 133–136
DOI: 10.2752/175174111X12954359478564
Reprints available directly from the Publishers.


# Letter from the Editors

Every so often we read in magazines or academic works about the global fashion centers of Paris, New York, London, Milan—their history, their unquestionable power, and how they function as vital hubs in far-reaching fashion systems. More recently, in the slipstream of globalization, the academic focus has turned to the world at large. The dominance of Western fashion has been questioned by fashion practices in the manufacturing countries outside the West, who were historically renowned for feeding exotic impulses into the fashions of Europe and North America. These studies have shattered the notion that there should be a single unified fashion history.

In this issue we follow this movement of decentering the study of fashion by turning the gaze to small European countries, which, although unquestionably belonging to "the West," have historically been marginal to the centralized dynamics of fashion. However, in recent years, a number of these countries have captured the attention of the international fashion press because of their designer fashion, sometimes engaging with distinctive cultural sources, sometimes with government support. In spite of their modest economic performance they have had a marked influence on national images and place-branding strategies. This themed issue brings together case studies of fashion design in Portugal, Holland, Belgium, Ireland, Iceland, Denmark, Norway, and Sweden. The first version of the papers was presented at a small conference at Copenhagen Business School in January 2010. We would like to take this opportunity to thank Creative Encounters for funding the event, Liselotte Skovsgaard Jessen and Maja Dueholm for organizing it, Kasper Eis of Dansk Fashion and Textile for a frank presentation of the dilemmas faced by a trade association trying to promote local designers, and the audience of students, teachers, and practitioners for contributing to a lively discussion.

All authors, except Norma Rantisi, are contributors to the *West Europe* volume of the *Berg Encyclopedia of World Dress and Fashion*, edited by Lise Skov (2010). This time we came together to explore a more narrowly focused problem of how the fashion worlds of small European countries have responded to recent globalization processes. The articles are intended to illustrate both similarities and differences, brought on by different geographies, histories, and societal structures. As Skov discusses in her introductory article, the rhetoric of new fashion centers can be seen as a traveling discourse that mobilizes people and organizations in different countries. She compares the emergent polycentric fashion system to the United Nations Security Council in which second-tier fashion centers can hold "the sixth seat," which gives them a temporal and regional constituency. Her central argument is that local designer fashion sectors contribute to the production of place through both promotional events and creative engagement with cultural resources.

José Teunissen's deconstruction of Belgian and Dutch fashion dreams analyzes some of the most successful designer fashion sectors in small European countries. In her comparison, which takes the Belgian success as its starting point to explore the less-known Dutch case, she finds a remarkable difference between the Belgian industry-driven promotion of the "Antwerp Six" and the Dutch designers' engagement first with the modernist tradition of design and classic painting and later also with regional dress and local crafts traditions.

Marie Riegels Melchior's article takes a comparative approach to the Scandinavian countries. She analyzes government involvement in the fashion sector—from the Danish endorsement of the fashion industry as a national success and promotional platform, by way of the industry-driven Swedish alliances between commerce and culture to the Norwegian dreams of national revival in the context of a more ethical industry. She argues that the Scandinavian countries have undergone a shift from design nations—in which the egalitarian principles of the social democratic welfare state were reflected in modernist design solutions—to fashion nations—replacing the commitment to social progress with the projection of changeable national images onto the international level.

"Creativity in the margins" is how Silé de Cléir summarizes her analysis of Irish fashion, thus emphasizing both the country's peripheral status vis-à-vis England and its ongoing active adaptation and appropriation of external influences. She uses the concept of "islands of identity" to conceptualize how aspects of global culture, as international fashion trends, are interpreted and re-created in a local context. Even during the current crisis she identifies a lively small-scale fashion culture, based, not only on the difference from neighboring England, but also on a rich tapestry of regional differences in taste within Ireland.

Portuguese fashion designers have yet to earn international attention, and Paula da Costa Soares shows that this is not for the lack of ambitious fashion designers. However, the development of Portuguese designer fashion has been restricted, historically, by the right-wing dictatorship that ruled the country until 1974, and since the 1990s, by the turn to fast fashion, aggressively promoted by the Spanish company Zara. In this respect, Soares argues that the goal of Portuguese fashion designers is not to be accepted as a new fashion center, but merely to stay in business.

The article by Æsa Sigurjónsdóttir is dedicated to Iceland, geographically situated on the northwestern edge of Europe, and remarkable for the way in which economic constraints seem to play a secondary role compared to the engagement with cultural identity. Singer, actress, and style icon Björk has played a central role in stimulating the local art and fashion scene, and indeed in shaping the national image of weirdness. But as Sigurjónsdóttir shows, Icelandic fashion designers are a motley crew, who seem to share only a strong sense of belonging to a place combined with a cosmopolitan vision of the trendy North.

Finally there are two short articles by Norma Rantisi and Simona Segre Reinach that serve as a commentary to the articles and overall theme. Rantisi focuses on the organizational set-up of second-tier fashion cities in post-manufacturing economies, pointing in particular to the importance of independent retailers in promoting small-scale designer brands, whereas Reinach takes a critical look at fashion designers' possibilities for international recognition under conditions of globalization.

The articles in this themed issue bring together multiple local histories of the moments and struggles of small-scale designer fashion sectors. They document the whole span of experiences between fashion's inscription in industry or government policy—a move that can carry fashion designers to triumph the international centers—and the stubborn resilience of local fashion dynamics, that continues in spite of closed factories and financial meltdowns. One of the critical findings, shared by all the authors, is that economic success is not a reliable indicator of the quality of fashion culture. Very often the most creative and meaningful local developments have taken place when the roads to Paris, London, Milan or New York have been blocked. For this reason, the experiences of small countries make a significant contribution to a more complete understanding of the rich and variegated world of fashion.

Lise Skov and Marie Riegels Melchior

## Reference

Skov, Lise (ed.). 2010. *Berg Encyclopedia of World Dress and Fashion*, Vol. 8, *West Europe*. Oxford: Berg.

*Fashion Theory*, Volume 15, Issue 2, pp. 137–156
DOI: 10.2752/175174111X12954359478609
Reprints available directly from the Publishers.
Photocopying permitted by licence only.

# Dreams of Small Nations in a Polycentric Fashion World

**Lise Skov**

Lise Skov is associate professor of creative industries at Copenhagen Business School. Educated as a sociologist in Denmark and Hong Kong, she has done extensive research on fashion industry and design in Japan, Hong Kong, and Europe. She is the editor of *West Europe*, Vol. 8 of *Berg Encyclopedia of World Dress and Fashion* (Berg, 2010).
ls.ikl@cbs.dk

## Abstract

Fashion production has been split between a globalized clothing industry, which tends towards extreme centralization, and localized designer fashion sectors, acting as intermediaries between international suppliers and national events, media, and public. Under these conditions, designer fashion takes on national significance, in terms of staging events and displays, and engaging with cultural references outside the field of fashion. This article explores how such place-making abilities structure the polycentric world of fashion, taking the United Nations Security Council as a model for the interaction between first- and second-tier

**fashion cities. The article analyzes the rhetoric of new fashion centers as a traveling discourse that detaches fashion design from the concerns of textile and clothing industries and links it with those of cultural institutions and governments. It also examines how notions of cultural superiority have held European designers back from giving local flavor to their designs, but how there has recently been an approximation between fashion and folk culture.**

**KEYWORDS: Europe, fashion design, identity, globalization, culture**

The transformation of the fashion system that took place in the second half of the twentieth century has been conceptualized by sociologists such as Gilles Lipovetsky (1994), Fred Davis (1992), and Diana Crane (2000) in the following way: whereas in the past, social distinction and class competition were the driving forces, fashion is now a mass phenomenon, commercially driven and addressing personal needs and desires. These scholars also hint that this transformation has had an effect on fashion's connection with place and nation, most clearly in Davis' argument that "the 'classic' centre-to-periphery framework" has been replaced by "fashion pluralism and polycentrism" (Davis 1992: 112). The present article is based on the assumption that the same conditions that have changed the way fashion organizes social structure—primarily the growing distance between producers and consumers and the increasing importance of images—have also facilitated a change in its organization of space, especially in its ability to endow certain places with an air of modernity and cosmopolitanism.

As a production system fashion has been split between a globalized clothing industry, which tends towards extreme centralization, and localized designer fashion sectors, acting as intermediaries between international suppliers and national events, media and public. What fashion designers can do for the nation today is not so much dress it—this is done by fast fashion operators in the global markets—but they can represent it, in what Richard Wilk has called "global structures of common difference" (2002). This has facilitated what I will call the place-making ability of fashion design—the ability to fill a cosmopolitan form with local content through displays and events associated with a heightened sense of here-and-now. So far, this has been studied mostly from the local perspective in a myriad of fashion histories. To complement these, the aim of this article is to clarify some of the general industrial, cultural, and governmental constraints and opportunities that have shaped the fashion trajectories of small European nations.

Since the 1980s, in particular, there has been an explosion in the rhetoric of new fashion centers. Countries and cities that in the past were content to see themselves as recipients of cosmopolitan clothing styles now claim to be style arbiters in their own right (Breward and Gilbert 2006). In a commentary on the booming of fashion weeks in all parts of the world, a *New York Times* headline reads, "The sun never sets on the catwalk" (September 7, 2008). This has made the travel schedule of the editors of the leading fashion magazines busier, but it has also increased the geographical and cultural variety of their contents. In the first decade of the twenty-first century this rhetoric reached the small nations in Europe. In Holland, a group of scholars received research funding to identify a Dutch fashion identity and history, in contrast to the dominant French style but also to the Belgian industry-driven fashion strategy of the 1990s. Denmark formulated its first fashion industry policy, as the ambitious dream of being the fifth fashion cluster in the world (less publicized was its starting point somewhere near the fifty-fifth position). And Reykjavik, the modest capital of one of Europe's smallest nations, was for some years considered to be a leading trend-setting city among designers and artists. Creativity has been written into Iceland's nation branding both in the expansive early years of the millennium, and in the recession after the financial collapse.

The old fashion centers, such as Paris, London, and New York, continue to exist, and hold an aggregate power that allows the capital city to dominate over the provinces, and even other countries, in terms of business and style. By comparison, the new fashion centers are not the leading business clusters that absorb the resources of a region and direct neighboring markets. Their contribution to national economies remains an open question. In this respect it may be argued that these new self-proclaimed fashion centers are not centers in any strict sense of the word. For example, they do not conform to Henri Lefebvre's notion of a center as something that pulls together diverse resources and is a place of decision-making (Lefebvre 1991: 332–3). They are oriented towards international validation, rather than domestic power. As we shall see, there is typically a sliding between whether it is a city or a nation that lays claim to being a fashion center. This marks a departure from fashion's long-standing association with cities (Gilbert 2006). However, the new fashion centers do reflect a third point of Lefebvre's analysis of space and centrality, the point that makes him one of the early scholars of globalization, the importance of being *included* in a macro-level transnational dynamics (Lefebvre 1991: 350).

I suggest the United Nations Security Council as an image for the relation between first- and second-tier fashion cities. The UN Security Council has five permanent members, the USA, Russia, the UK, and France—the four allied powers of World War II—and China. In addition, non-permanent membership is rotated between all other nations, which are elected for two-year periods. Non-permanent membership of the UN Security Council is referred to as "the sixth seat," and it is considered to be a special opportunity and responsibility when a small nation has the chance to sit at the same table and negotiate directly with the superpowers. What is less publicized is the fact that the UN Security Council has ten non-permanent members at any given time, representing different regional blocs. Thus the "sixth seat" is not a unique position, but one held by ten nations at the same time. To transfer this image to fashion, the "sixth seat" thus represents what is possible for small nations in the polycentric fashion world. They can achieve international renown, but they are tied to a temporal and regional constituency.

The word "dreams" in the title has two overlapping meanings. Firstly, it is intended as a cover-all term for what is a diverse set of initiatives, policies, and plans, many of which are discussed in the case studies presented in the following articles in this issue. Thus the "dream" brings together individual fashion designers bringing culturally significant inspiration into his or her collections, the trade association's organization of catwalk shows or an overseas trade mission, the municipality's city branding strategy, and the magazines' write-up of global and local stories. The term also lumps together cultural creativity with marketing and industry strategies, the common denominator being that all these diverse phenomena express the notion that local fashion design is of international standard, and somehow significant for the city or nation.

Secondly, "dream" is used to capture an imaginary and expressive quality of many of the initiatives. This reflects not only their aspirational character—the ambition of making it on the international stage, but also the remaking of the local through new visions and perceptions. The implicit argument here is that this is a phenomenon that cannot be adequately understood through an industry analysis alone. It must be interpreted through a culturally sensitive framework, which allows for a rather loose, non-functionalistic dreamlike connection between diverse elements.

The organization of the article is as follows: in the first section I analyze the new fashion center phenomenon as a traveling discourse, which was formed on the basis of the international success of Japanese fashion designers in the 1980s, and has since been taken up in Asia before in recent years becoming active in small nations in Europe. Then I go on to discuss the new requirement that fashion design must engage with cultural sources outside the field of fashion. In relation to European fashion designers this represents both an obstacle (due to a deep-seated perception that fashion is the opposite of national culture), and an opportunity for localizing fashion design. In the third section, I take a closer look at the place-making ability that has become central to what fashion designers produce. One of the findings is that local fashion dynamics are resilient even in the time of economic crisis.

## The Formation of a Traveling Discourse

The notion of a traveling discourse was developed by cultural studies scholars, such as Partha Chatterjee (1985) and Edward Said (1994), to conceptualize the power of nationalism in non-Western countries in the early part of the twentieth century. In its transnational circulation, a traveling discourse engages people, industries, and governments, mobilizes resources, and shapes national dreams. Thus, a traveling discourse unites global diffusion and cultural imperialism with local development and national autonomy. But while Chatterjee's traveling discourse led to the building of industrial economies and modern infrastructure, the new traveling discourse communicates demands brought on by increasing globalization, deindustrialization, and the turn to "immaterial" production, conceptualized through terms such as intellectual property, design, and creative industries (Wang 2004).

To clarify what I mean by the distinction between old and new fashion centers it is instructive to compare Milan and Tokyo fashion designers. Both have been internationally successful—the Italian designers in the 1970s and 1980s; the Japanese in the 1980s in particular. But there is a qualitative difference. The success of Milan was based on a particular business model—that of the entrepreneur-designer—exemplified by Giorgio Armani, Gianfranco Ferré, and Mariuccia Mandelli behind the label Krizia. According to Simona Segre Reinach (2010), Milan was a hub that drew together industrial networks with professionals in art and media in an atmosphere of cosmopolitan open-mindedness. This enabled a mix of artisanal creativity and technology on the one hand, and sophisticated image-based distribution and marketing on the other. Although by now the business model has been undermined by the globalization of clothing manufacturing, it is still associated with Milan through the city's consumer culture and also through subsequent generations of fashion designers for whom it represents a cultural resource.

By contrast, when we look at Japan, the roots of its success seem to spread in all directions. Firstly, it is based on international acknowledgment of a series of fashion designers—most notably the "Big Three": Issey Miyake, Yohji Yamamoto, and Rei Kawakubo of Comme des Garçons. To be sure, their work was embedded in Japanese business models and industry networks. But their success was established as much in Paris as at home (Kawamura 2004; Skov 1996). Secondly, it is significant that in the same period as Japanese designers were celebrated as the greatest innovators of international fashion, the country had become the major importer of European luxury goods. Japan was never a passive emulator of Western taste, and it was the adaptation to its demanding consumer market that set Louis Vuitton and similar companies on the track of the commercialization strategies that led to their phenomenal sales in the first decade of the twenty-first century (Goodrum 2009; Hata 2004; Thomas 2007). Thirdly, the long-term influence that Japan has exercised on international fashion comes neither from its avant-garde brands, nor from its consumer markets, but from the youth subcultures for whom dress is particularly significant (Keet 2007).

In addition to these discrepancies between the Japanese industry and consumer markets, the Western fashion press wrote up the success of

Japanese designers using a proliferation of cultural references from outside the field of fashion. Without much care about facilitating a sober understanding of a new phenomenon the fashion press gorged on images that enforced Japan's otherness from the West—images that seemed to contradict the industrial development, urbanization, and sophisticated consumer market, which were the very conditions for the international breakthrough. Dorinne Kondo (1997) criticized the essentialism and stereotypes that tainted Japan's moment as a global style leader. I tried to show the ambiguity in an international acknowledgment that is so closely tied to cultural distinctiveness. The external recognition seems to have overdetermined the local dynamics. It presents a new kind of design dilemma of how to balance cosmopolitan trends with local content (Skov 2003).

Compared to Milan fashion, it is impossible to distill out of the Japanese globalization experience a specific business model, or even a coordination of industry, media, and consumers. Neither can its success be measured in economic terms through sales or export figures. The Japanese success marked a detachment of the production and consumption of fashion clothing from media and images, a tendency which, as we shall see, had by no means reached its end point in the 1980s. An element of this trend is the sliding between the city and the nation, made possible by the fact that so many of the significant events took place either on the international scene, at Paris Fashion Week, or in the pages of international fashion magazines.

It would be hard to overestimate the role of Japan in defining the discourse of new fashion centers. But just as the experience of Japanese fashion designers was contradictory, so were the lessons that other nations drew from their international success. Its Asian neighbors were the first to translate the Japanese success into industry strategies to upgrade their highly developed export-based textile and clothing industries. Thus governments, industries, and schools in Korea, Thailand, Taiwan, Hong Kong, and subsequently the People's Republic of China, have supported groups of name designers who could match international trends with culturally distinctively styles. Through their research into, and creative engagement with, national and traditional aesthetics, fashion designers began to produce multiple versions of fashion styles that were at the same time cosmopolitan and non-Western. As such they spoke to a long-standing cultural debate of modernity and difference, while at the same time contributing to legitimizing Asian popular culture internationally (Skov 2003, 2004).

By contrast, Europeans have only slowly picked up on the potential associated with culturally distinctive styles. The first Europeans to emulate the Japanese success were the Belgians who, in a bold move to revitalize their struggling textile and clothing industry, employed a group of newly graduated designers for an international promotion in the 1980s

(Bronselaer 2010). The notion of the "Antwerp Six" echoes the "Big Three," but whereas the three Japanese designers represented those who had proven themselves as the best in a much larger field of viable name designer companies, the six Belgians were young designers selected to participate in the international mission, and given the first chance to start up their own businesses. From the "Big Three," they also took an intellectually probing approach to dressmaking, working with new ways of cutting and stitching and using materials, thus consolidating the movement of Deconstructionism in fashion design. This, however, was done in a culturally neutral style (see also Teunissen, this issue).

In all the cases discussed so far, textile and clothing industries were the driving forces. The reason for this is that the clothing industry, an extremely competitive labor-intensive sector, is highly globalized. Industries in the most developed countries, including Northwest Europe and Japan, have been on a long-term decline since the early 1970s, when domestic production began to be replaced by imports from low-wage countries. At first this benefited a wide range of developing countries, most notably Hong Kong, Korea, and Taiwan. But since the emergence in the 1980s of China and India as major manufacturing economies, these industries have also been on the decline. The European Union has created its own regional geography of fashion production. When Portugal and Spain joined the EU in the 1980s they became favored manufacturing countries for the wholesalers and brand owners in Northern Europe. A similar role has more recently been taken by the East European countries that joined the EU in 2004. But even in these manufacturing regions, increasing wages threaten to erode their international competitiveness almost from the day the clusters are established. For all these industries, fashion design has at some point or other represented a means of upgrading their production in order to increase its value and sustain higher wages, thereby lengthening the lifetime of the regional industry.

As Karlijn Bronselaer (2010: 202) points out, investing in fashion design is also a way for the textile and clothing industries to address an "image problem," brought about both by the conditions of labor-intensive manufacturing and by the typical products of export-oriented suppliers—good and reliable in quality, but perceived as stagnant and boring. Supporting fashion designers—either through long-term backing, which is the typical set-up of the Japanese industry, or through short-term events, such as the shows of the Antwerp Six, which were presented at home as well as abroad—can thus be a strategy to associate the clothing industry with the creativity and dynamism it otherwise seems to lack. It is in this vein that Hong Kong has presented itself as an up-and-coming fashion center since the 1960s when export garments began to grow, and that a recent initiative for a new European fashion union came from the provincial Bulgarian city of Brasov.

But in the nations where the textile and clothing sector has been almost completely deindustrialized there has also been a growth in the rhetoric of new fashion centers. This increasing detachment from branded clothes production marks a qualitative step in the discourse of new fashion centers that brings it in closer alignment with the highly volatile sector constituted by young fashion designers' very small and highly unstable companies, operating in what Angela McRobbie has called a mixed economy of commercial earnings and public support, including unemployment benefits (McRobbie 1998: 89). It is significant that she presents young London fashion designers as stretched out between the glamorous magazine world of fashion and the educational discourses of the art school, but only marginally connected to the industry, and then only with small-scale urban suppliers (1998: 14). The rationale for governments to value such a small and fragmented sector is neither economic, nor cultural, as an inherently worthy artistic production, but a combination of the two. In the UK policy for creative industries, designer fashion (though not the fashion sector as a whole) is included among the other creative industries that are characterized by their ability to transform individual creativity into money-making potential (Hesmondhalgh 2008). A variation on the same theme is Richard Florida's notion that the presence of a creative class makes a city attractive for highly skilled labor, and in turn an attractive location for large companies (2004). According to this logic, a municipality that wishes to ensure a strong economy first of all needs to stimulate the creative sector.

The detachment of enterprise from fashion designers is thus increased to the point that the connection is almost purely symbolic. We might even be able to extend the notion of a traveling discourse to a discourse that not only travels from nation to nation, but that has even migrated from its own industry to find new functions, goals, and stakeholders (Breward and Gilbert 2006). Thus the drivers of the designer fashion sector in the deindustrialized countries and cities are governments, design schools, media, the arts, and other creative industries, as well as cultural institutions such as museums. Fashion designers may be a part of the creative underground and, perceived as artists, they are increasingly eligible for the kinds of government subsidies that characterize the cultural sectors in European nations. This change is illustrated by the trajectory of Belgian fashion from the ambitious textile plan of the early 1980s to the consolidation of Antwerp as a fashion city, centered on the ModeNatie (Fashion Nation) building, which is home to a couple of designer flagship stores along with the network organization Flanders Fashion Institute, a design school, MoMu fashion museum, a book store, and a coffee shop. The focus is no longer on industry development, but on providing knowledge and experiences, especially for the tourists who are attracted by the notion of Flanders as a creative region.

## Europe and the Challenge of Making Fashion Culturally Distinctive

The traveling discourse of new fashion centers presents fashion designers with a dilemma: on the one hand, they must show that even though they come from peripheral cities such as Antwerp, Dublin, Oslo or Porto, their collections are of an international standard. On the other hand, they must use the cosmopolitan code of fashion to present something distinctive and place-bound that sets them apart from the rest of the fashion scene. This was also the design dilemma faced by Hong Kong fashion designers whom in previous research I described as balancing the pulls of globalization and localization (Skov 2003: 241). In the 1990s, Hong Kong fashion designers engaged in a kind of collective project of searching for inspiration outside the conventional field of fashion, avoiding cultural stereotypes by making sure their version of the local was not obvious, and finally, commenting on other designers' work, often in a critical and competitive spirit (Figure 1).

In as far as this design dilemma was first experienced in Japan, and then migrated to a series of Asian countries, it is pertinent to ask why it has taken so long before it became recognized as a common condition for European fashion designers. For example, in spite of their international success, the Belgian designers have not endorsed the idea that cultural distinctiveness should give a new fashion center a competitive edge. A part of the explanation must be found in the fact that Belgium, one of the youngest nations in West Europe, is deeply divided between French-speaking Wallonia in the South and Dutch-speaking Flanders in the North. By the early 1990s, it was impossible to sustain a nationally

**Figure 1**
In the 1990s in Hong Kong, there was a collective ambition to develop fashion collections that were at the same time up to international standard and locally meaningful. With the permission of the Hong Kong Trade Development Council.

coordinated industry policy; in the first decade of the twenty-first century the divide has led to a string of political crises. In this respect, both Hong Kong and Belgium are instructive (negative) cases that illustrate the power of a legitimate nation state today to go deep into people's sense of belonging and permanence.

But the Belgian story also reveals a more general reluctance on the part of Europeans to see themselves as one piece in the "fruitful diversity of the world's cultures" to use the term inscribed in UNESCO's constitution (UNESCO 2009). Instead, Europe has often perceived itself as a kind of utopia or an unattainable ideal. In this sense, it designates not merely a geographical region, but the top position in the hierarchy of civilization—a position at odds with the religious persecution, violent colonization, and totalitarian contempt for human life that have also characterized European history. British historian Norman Davies has defined Eurocentrism as the traditional tendency of European authors to regard their culture as superior and self-contained, and to neglect to take non-European viewpoints into consideration. It is manifest in multiple works about Europe, written by Europeans and for Europeans, with the assumption that Europe constitutes an example that non-Europeans would wish to follow (Davies 1997: 16).

He further argues that Eurocentrism also operates within Europe's own regions. For example, he criticizes scholars who take the West or Western civilization as a key concept, and who write as if they represented a single unified viewpoint. The tradition for focusing on the "great powers" at the expense of the "small nations," which jointly make up the European tapestry, stems from the nineteenth century. In the twentieth century the West moved to an imaginary transatlantic site, assuming a unity between Europe and North America. In each case, diversity, which is one of Europe's enduring features, is ignored. In contrast to such reductive analyses, Davies presents the need for describing Europe in its entirety. He calls for the multiplicity of small stories to be brought into the big history, by including Portugal, Ireland, Scotland and Wales, Scandinavia, as well as Poland, Hungary, Bohemia, Byzantium, Balkans, Baltic States, Belorussia, Ukraine, Crimea, and Caucasus (Davies 1997: 19).

The conventional history of fashion has been in alignment with the Eurocentrism that Davies criticizes. For example, rather than fashion being seen as a single instance of universal strategies of change, it has been perceived to have originated and developed exclusively in Europe, embodying cultural superiority, firstly, in the perceived civilized appearance vis-à-vis the uncivilized primitiveness that non-Western dress was supposed to represent, and secondly, in its association with dynamism and progress vis-à-vis the perceived stability and slowness of non-Western dress. Sandra Niessen shows that not only is such a dualistic conceptual system incorrect, but its "ideological blinkers" have "stymied inquiry into the possibility of alternative systems of fashion and dress and the exploration of such issues as mechanisms of change in alternative systems" (Niessen 2010: 43).

The recently published *Berg Encyclopedia of World Dress and Fashion* aims to redress the imbalance that results from the privileging of the West in the ten geographically organized volumes, conceptualized and edited by anthropologist Joanne B. Eicher (2010). Building on Norman Davies' point that Eurocentrism is also at work in Europe, the volume on West Europe, which I edited, and which carries articles by all the contributors (except Rantisi) to this themed issue, speaks to this project by bringing together country articles that documents different national trajectories and reflects national research traditions of the small nations side by side with those of the "great powers." In this respect, the volume illustrates that Europe's cultural identity, in the words of Italian novelist Alberto Moravia, is "a reversible fabric, one side variegated ... the other a single colour, rich and deep" (quoted in Davies 1997: 10).

The countries covered in this themed issue—Iceland, Portugal, Ireland, Norway, Sweden, Denmark, Holland, and Belgium—many of which are included in Davies's list—have all experienced themselves as off-center recipients of stylistic influences from the old fashion capitals of Paris and London. Yet, on closer examination, the geographical power structures are too variable to be fitted into a single center-to-periphery framework. The most obvious example is Ireland, in so many ways dwarfed by its dominant neighbor. Yet as de Cléir documents, there have been continuous local fashion dynamics, not only in the eighteenth and nineteenth century, but also in what she terms "Dublin's moment" in the 1950s, and in contemporary media and blogging. The latter point shows that even if the virtue of the Internet is mostly perceived to be its ability to transcend distance, local dynamics are also reinscribed in the new technology when language, the dominant anchor of identity in Europe, does not draw the boundaries. In a similar vein, Soares analyzes the existence of Portuguese designer fashion in the shadow of the Spanish fast fashion industry, although her conclusion is more pessimistic about the Portuguese designers' ability to hold on to a commercially viable market. In her discussion of Scandinavia, Melchior uncovers a subdued rivalry between Copenhagen and Stockholm as to which city can claim to be the fashion leader of the region.

For a moment I wish to go back to the creative dilemma faced by the designers. In their search for local inspiration outside the field of legitimate fashion it is clear that they can go in different directions. Jennifer Craik outlines one direction in her analysis of Australian fashion by focusing on dress associated with Australian lifestyle—"bush" wear, surf, and swimwear, as well as indigenous design (2009). In this respect, what she terms national dress is associated with popular activities and culture. Indeed, popular culture is in many ways the natural "home" for fashion, as shown by multiple studies of street style and subculture. An example of a newly established fashion brand that consciously draws on elements of popular culture outside the realm of fashion is the Norwegian Moods of Norway (Figure 2). As an ironic reference to Ralph Lauren's logo with horse and polo player, Moods of Norway sports a tractor logo, thus reversing the claim of a leisured life in the country to that of the monotonous outdoor work of the country bumpkin. With loud colors, busy patterns, and synthetic materials the brand carries retro references to provincial Norwegians' first encounter with postwar affluence of the 1950s and 1960s.

Another strategy is to model fashion design on high culture and art. This approach is typical of Vivienne Westwood, one of a few British designers with a culturally distinctive approach. Suffused with irony, she has picked her sources of inspiration from national symbols and upper-class lifestyle, whether the Union Jack, reworked by punk, or the queen and the landed gentry that have had a central role her later collections. The approach of borrowing from art can also be applied to the work process, for example, by adapting the deconstructionist methods

**Figure 2**
Moods of Norway, founded in 2003, typifies a new European attitude to the use of national references in fashion design and branding. Photograph: Ole Musken. With the permission of Moods of Norway.

of intellectual analysis to clothing design, as the Belgian designers did. Another example is Dutch designer Alexander van Slobbe's notion of abstraction that he deducted from the traditions of Flemish art and craft (see Teunissen, this issue). Interestingly, van Slobbe credits his search for a Dutch approach to fashion to the cultural expectations he was met with when he was working in Japan (van den Berg 2008). This illustrates the ongoing influence of Japan in shaping the parameters of polycentric fashion.

While the axis between high and low culture is familiar territory for fashion design, folk culture—the third position in the tripartite model of culture—accentuates the design dilemma. For many fashion designers, this brings out a fear of overdoing cultural stereotypes, exacerbated by the common perception that folk culture is the opposite of fashion—rural, static, backward, and soaked in nationalism. The discomfort many Europeans feel with this kind of self-exoticization is ironic because fashion in the twentieth century, with its long-standing tradition for exoticism, has had no qualms about incorporating all kinds of colorful elements from non-Western, including Russian, folk culture. The new demand is that designers engage with their national culture and dress tradition, but in such a way that it can be attractive to outsiders.

In this respect, the recent softening of the perceived boundaries between fashion and folk dress—felt in both Moods of Norway and Alexander van Slobbe—illustrates how far fashion design has come in its engagement with the symbols of national culture. Nordic folk dress scholars have used the term "revitalization" to signify "the process of restoring or recreating a phenomenon from the past in relation to the conditions of the present" to understand the difference between the traditional preindustrial use of rural dress, and the ceremonial and symbolic role national dress has had in the modern period (Haugen 2010: 18). Perhaps we can extend this concept to cover the revitalization of folk dress in relation to contemporary fashion design? This is a revitalization that takes folk dress out of its ceremonial use, which symbolizes membership of a national community, into an eclectic mix 'n' match use that symbolizes a cosmopolitan appreciation of different cultures.

Historically, the central aspect of folk dress has been its dependence on locally available resources in terms of materials, processing, and craftsmanship. By engaging with this part of the tradition, fashion's interface with folk dress can be a step towards a more sustainable production, by facilitating new designs and markets for local manufacturing systems, already minimized by global competition. An example of this is the revitalization of woolen knitwear that been so important for culture and industry in Iceland (discussed by Sigurjónsdóttir, this issue), Ireland (discussed by de Cléir, this issue), and other nations facing the North Atlantic.

## From Dressmaking to Place Making

If, as I stated in the beginning of this article, the changes from "the 'classic' centre-to-periphery framework" to "fashion pluralism and polycentrism" (Davis 1992) constitute a transformation of the fashion system, it becomes relevant to ask the question: what do fashion designers actually produce? If fashion is characterized by its ability to create a heightened sense of here-and-now, then we can say that it has turned its ability to make staccato marks in social space from the seasonal launching of novelties to an ongoing launching of different cities as fresh and trendy. This is done not only through the design strategies discussed above, but also through events staged for display and sales. In relation to the traveling discourse of new fashion centers, we can narrow down the question to: what do fashion designers produce that is significant for the nation?

In answering this question it is necessary to remember how difficult it used to be to connect fashion and nation in a meaningful way. Numerous works referenced in this article (including my own) comment on how the combination of the word "fashion" with "Belgium" or "Australia" or "Hong Kong" is unfamiliar and remarkable. It is less than thirty years since British historians Eric Hobsbawm and Terence Ranger coined the term "the invention of tradition" (1983) in a criticism that showed that claims to authenticity, made by romantic and cultural nationalists in the nineteenth century, were manufactured relatively recently. But the argument such as the one made by Hugh Trevor-Roper (1983) that the Scottish kilt only dates back to the eighteenth century, and probably comes from England, really only has critical force if we buy into the ideal of cultural superiority and self-containment—as Davies pointed out, the key elements of Eurocentrism. If the old nationalism, criticized by Hobsbawn, Ranger, and Trevor-Roper, was characterized by the claim that the nation is primordial, ancient, and unchanging—in short the antithesis of fashion, then the new nationalism, signified by the traveling discourse of creative industries and new fashion centers, does the opposite: it rejuvenates the nation and shows that it is open to the world.

This also marks a change in the national political project from the early twentieth century with its focus on building of industrial economies and modern infrastructure to the post-industrial concern with international attractiveness. As Melchior points out (this issue), cultural identity is increasingly seen as a component in national competitiveness as creative capability. The new nationalism views the nation more like a renewable resource that can be reinvented in interaction with global changes. Orvar Löfgren has coined the term the "catwalk economy" for the highly choreographed release of novelty, conducted through events and ritualized display (2005). Product launches are surrounded by an atmosphere of excitement and chaos that helps everybody forget that in a few months today's new version can be found on the sales racks. Löfgren sees this as a generalized feature that the new economy has taken over from *haute couture*'s system of biannual collections. Melchior *et al.* (2011) argue that the catwalk economy is reproduced at the national level. This, at least, is the case in Denmark where the government has taken a keen interest in the fashion industry and made it a paradigm for economic success under conditions of deindustrialization. Thus, ironically, the industry that is famous for endorsing laissez-faire liberalism has been the first to receive government support under the new program for creative industries.

The case studies presented in this issue range from the policy-driven examples—among which Denmark stands out for the way in which the economic success of the fashion industry has been taken up by government organizations and individual politicians for their own purposes—to those characterized by economic failure, in particular Ireland and Iceland. In between are countries such as the Netherlands, Sweden, Norway, and Portugal, in which the designer fashion sectors have developed, more or less successfully, with a more or less solid network of government, manufacturing systems, consumer markets, and cultural organizations. In Ireland, recent developments take place against the bleak backdrop of the dismantling of the manufacturing industry, leaving politicians, industrialists, and designers alike disillusioned about any kind of future for Irish fashion. In contrast to the special subsidies that fall to the Danish industry, the Irish trade association, struggling with the image of a crisis-ridden sunset industry, argues against policies that discriminate between individual sectors. Nevertheless, the growth in local fashion weeks and independent boutiques shows that the resilience of local fashion dynamics has little to do with economic trends (see de Cléir, this issue). The same can be said for Iceland where after the financial meltdown in 2008, the art and fashion scene has been reinvigorated by small enterprises, founded by young people who lost their jobs during the crisis, pop-up markets in abandoned shops, and Internet-based social network sites (see Sigurjónsdóttir, this issue).

To round off this section, I wish to take a look at different success criteria that have been used to evaluate different local initiatives. The first criterion is economic. However, as the new fashion center phenomenon is increasingly detached from industry concerns, it can be misleading to evaluate their success in the context of industry performance. Indeed, fashion may seem to be a somewhat arbitrary headline for an industrial sector that comprises all kinds of garments, including childrenswear, underwear, workwear and sportswear, and textiles, including textiles for interior and functionality (Dutch textile giant TenCate is a major supplier of artificial turf), and even agricultural byproducts such as leather and fur (which boost Danish fashion exports). Also, in deindustrialized countries, export figures are based on re-exports rather than on manufacturing, so it is hard to connect them in any direct way with local creativity.

Perhaps a more appropriate success criterion is global connectivity? This better captures the dual pulls of globalization and localization. For a small nation, the international success of a few individual designers in Paris, London or New York can be of enormous importance, not only symbolically, but also because they act as conducting wires between the local and the global. Examples are Dutch fashion forecaster Li Edelkoort, founder of one of the influential French trend bureaux in 1975, Danish former supermodel Helena Christensen, based in New York, where, among other things, she runs a boutique that stocks Danish brands, or Icelandic performance artist Bjork who has initiated and commissioned numerous avant-garde projects in Icelandic fashion, design and art, and whose personal vision has influenced the national branding. Another aspect of global connectivity is the ability to capture the attention of the international fashion press. Often extreme effort is put into soliciting editors of leading fashion magazines in New York, London, and Tokyo to visit second-tier fashion weeks, and ensuring easy transportation from fashion show to fashion show (Skov and Meier 2011). Attracting tourists is also an aspect of global connectivity, which although it goes outside the professional networks of fashion, is often an attractive success criterion for municipalities and cultural institutions, such as museums, which have found that fashion exhibitions can attract not only crowds of enthusiastic visitors, but also corporate sponsorship.

To this we need to add a third success criterion that evaluates the quality of the local dynamics. Like economic performance and global connectivity, this is also a slippery success criterion. But it enables us to evaluate the difference between the political overdetermination of the activities of fashion companies and designers in Denmark—which borders on the *un*-making of a place—with the liveliness of small-scale fashion dynamics in Ireland and Iceland. The latter are reminiscent of Hong Kong fashion designers of the 1990s who, finding their way into international fashion blocked, redirected their energy towards local conditions, thus turning into astute cultural commentators at home (Skov 2003: 234). Enrichment of local participatory culture, and critical and creative reflection of common values and ideals through fashion design, hinge upon new organizational networks of designers, with artists, scholars, grass-root politicians, and business entrepreneurs. Local developments are particularly important since new fashion centers typically find it impossible to sustain international attention. Ultimately, it is at the local level that small nations' designer fashion sectors can have a lasting impact.

## Conclusion

By way of conclusion I wish to pull the focus back from the local to the global. The multiple local initiatives and dynamics, which have been discussed here, may indicate that the old notion of fashion centers has been replaced by complete fragmentation, akin to UNESCO's model of the world as a mosaic of equal inherently worthy cultures. However, under the global gaze, a patterned order is still visible. I describe it with reference to another United Nations organization—the Security Council (Figure 3).

Just as the superpowers dominate the UN Security Council, so the old fashion centers—Paris, London, Milan, New York, and Tokyo—still hold absolutely dominant positions in terms of both business and the imaginary in the polycentric fashion world. But their reign is supplemented by a circulation of what Norma Rantisi and Deborah Leslie have termed second-tier, or not-so-global fashion cities (2006). Their range of operation is mostly regional, even though they may capture global attention for a limited period of time. The model of the UN Security Council thus tempers the goals that second-tier fashion cities can hope to attain. New fashion centers have a constituency that is regional and temporal. International recognition is not the first step to ongoing expansion for an up-and-coming fashion center, but rather its fifteen minutes of fame.

Saying that second-tier fashion cities hold "the sixth seat" is a statement about their orientation towards the superpowers of fashion, rather than towards their peers. Their relation to other not-so-global cities is characterized more by competition than collaboration, and more by willful ignorance than mutual acknowledgment. The closest we get to an organization like the UN Security Council in fashion is the leading magazines with editorial offices in Paris, London, New York, and Tokyo. They now include stories of second-tier fashion cities, but these are secondary to those from the global fashion centers, and the number of second-tier cities that can make it are restrained both by the editors' travel schedule and by the limited number of pages given over to new fashion cities. Of course the polycentric world of fashion is not a formal

**Figure 3**
Is the sixth seat in the UN Security Council analogous to what small nations can achieve in the polycentric fashion world? Photograph: UN Photo/Paulo Filgueiras.

organization with institutionalized turn-taking. The second-tier fashion cities have to jostle for attention, in an environment marked by changeability and uncertainty.

Building on the studies of scholars such as Lipovetsky (1994), Crane (2000), and Davis (1992), I wish to suggest that the changeability of fashion that they have analyzed in relation to dress and class has been magnified and projected onto the planet so that it is at play in relation to nations and international competition. This has been made possible by the globalization, both of the fashion sectors—which have detached local industries from constraints of garment manufacturing—and of the whole national economies—which has made global connectivity a key competitive parameter. Also at this global level, we can apply Georg Simmel's point that faithless changeability is one of fashion's democratic characteristics—because it ensures that no advantage is permanent (1923). These days, nations and cities also go in and out of fashion.

## References

Breward, Christopher and David Gilbert (eds). 2006. *Fashion's World Cities*. Oxford: Berg.

Bronselaer, Karlijn. 2010. "Belgium." In Lise Skov (ed.) *Berg Encyclopedia of World Dress and Fashion*, Vol. 8, *West Europe*, pp. 199–204. Oxford: Berg.

Chatterjee, Partha. 1985. *National Thought and the Colonial World*. London: Zed Books.

Craik, Jennifer. 2009. "Is Australian Fashion and Dress Distinctively Australian?" *Fashion Theory* 13(4): 409–42.

Crane, Diana 2000. *Fashion and Its Social Agendas: Class, Gender and Identity in Clothing*. Chicago, IL: University of Chicago Press.

Davies, Norman. 1997. *Europe: A History*. London: Pimlico.

Davis, Fred. 1992. *Fashion, Culture and Identity*. Chicago, IL: University of Chicago Press.

Eicher, Joanne (ed.). 2010. *Berg Encyclopedia of World Dress and Fashion*. Oxford: Berg.

Florida, Richard. 2004. *The Rise of the Creative Class*. New York: Basic Books.

Gilbert, David. 2006. "From Paris to Shanghai: The Changing Geographies of Fashion's World Cities." In Christopher Breward and David Gilbert (eds) *Fashion's World Cities*, pp. 3–32. Oxford: Berg.

Goodrum, Alison. 2009. "True Brits? Authoring National Identity in Anglo-Japanese Fashion Exports." *Fashion Theory* 13(4): 461–80.

Hata, Kyojiro. 2004. *Louis Vuitton Japan: The Building of Luxury*. New York: Assouline.

Haugen, Bjørn Sverre Hol. 2010. "The Concept of Dress in the Nordic Countries." In Lise Skov (ed.) *Berg Encyclopedia of World Dress and Fashion*, Vol. 8, *West Europe*, pp. 18–22. Oxford: Berg.

Hesmondhalgh, David. 2008. "Cultural and Creative Industries." T. Bennett and J. Frow (eds) *The SAGE Handbook of Cultural Analysis*, pp. 552–69. Los Angeles, CA: Sage.

Hobsbawm, Eric and Terence Ranger (eds). 1983. *The Invention of Tradition*. Cambridge: Cambridge University Press.

Kawamura, Yuniya. 2004. *The Japanese Revolution in Paris Fashion*. Oxford: Berg.

Keet, Philomena. 2007. *The Tokyo Look Book*. Tokyo: Kodansha.

Kondo, Dorinne. 1997. *About Face: Performing Race in Fashion and Theater*. New York: Routledge.

Lefebvre, Henri .1991. *The Production of Space*. Oxford: Blackwell.

Lipovetsky, Gilles. 1994. *The Empire of Fashion: Dressing Modern Democracy*. Princeton, NJ: Princeton University Press.

Löfgren, Orvar. 2005. "Catwalking and Coolhunting: The Production of Newness." In Orvar Löfgren and Robert Willim (eds) *Magic, Culture and the New Economy*, pp. 57–71. Oxford: Berg.

McRobbie, Angela. 1998. *British Fashion Design: Rag Trade or Image Industry?* London: Routledge.

Melchior, Marie Riegels, Lise Skov and Fabian Csaba. 2011. "Translating Fashion into Danish." *Culture Unbound* 3: XX–XX.

Niessen, Sandra. 2010. "Interpreting 'Civilization' through Dress." In Lise Skov (ed.) *Berg Encyclopedia of World Dress and Fashion*, Vol. 8, *West Europe*, pp. 39–43. Oxford: Berg.

Rantisi, Norma and Deborah Leslie. 2006. "Branding the Design Metropole: The Case of Montréal, Canada." *Area* 38(4): 364–76.

Reinach, Simona Segre. 2010. "Milan as a Fashion City." In Liswe Skov (ed.) *Berg Encyclopedia of World Dress and Fashion*, Vol. 8, *West Europe*, pp. 259–63. Oxford: Berg.

Said, Edward. 1994. *Culture and Imperialism*. New York: Vintage Books.

Simmel, Georg. 1923. "Die Mode." In *Philosophische Kultur*, pp. 38–63. Berlin: Wagenbach.

Skov, Lise. 1996. "Fashion Trends, Japonisme and Postmodernism, or 'What is so Japanese about *Comme des Garçons*?'" *Theory, Culture and Society* 13(3): 129–51.

Skov, Lise. 2003. "Fashion-Nation: A Japanese Globalization Experience and a Hong Kong Dilemma." In Carla Jones, Ann Marie Leshkowich and Sandra Niessen (eds) *Re-Orienting Fashion: The Globalization of Asian Fashion*, pp. 215–43. Oxford: Berg.

Skov, Lise. 2004. "Fashion Flows—Fashion Shows: The Asia-Pacific Meets in Hong Kong." In Koichi Iwabuchi and Mandy Thomas (eds.) *Rogue Flows: Trans-Asian Cultural Traffic*, pp. 221–47. Hong Kong: Hong Kong University Press.

Skov, Lise (ed.). 2010. *Berg Encyclopedia of World Dress and Fashion*, Vol. 8, *West Europe*. Oxford: Berg.

Skov, Lise and Janne Meier. 2011. "Configuring Sustainability at Fashion Week." In Brian Moeran and Jesper Strandgaard Pedersen (eds) *Negotiating Values in the Creative Industries*, pp. XX–XX. Cambridge: Cambridge University Press.

Thomas, Dana. 2007. *De Luxe: How Luxury Lost Its Luster.* New York: Penguin Press.

Trevor-Roper, Hugh. 1983. "The Invention of Tradition: The Highland Tradition of Scotland." In Eric Hobsbawm and Terence Ranger (eds) *The Invention of Tradition*, pp. 15–42. Cambridge: Cambridge University Press.

UNESCO. 2009. *Investing in Cultural Diversity and Intercultural Dialogue*. New York: UNESCO World Report 2.

Van den Berg, Nanda. 2008. *Alexander van Slobbe*. Harderwijk/Arnhem: D'jonge Hond/ArtEZ Press.

Wang, Jing. 2004. "The Global Reach of a New Discourse: How Far Can 'Creative Industries' Travel?" *International Journal of Cultural Studies* 7(1): 1–19.

Wilk, Richard. 2002. "Television, Time, and the National Imaginary in Belize." In Faye D. Ginsburg, Lila Abu-Lughod and Brian Larkin (eds) *Media Worlds*, pp. 171–86. Berkeley, CA: University of California Press.

*Fashion Theory,* Volume 15, Issue 2, pp. 157–176
DOI: 10.2752/175174111X12954359478645
Reprints available directly from the Publishers.
Photocopying permitted by licence only.

# Deconstructing Belgian and Dutch Fashion Dreams: From Global Trends to Local Crafts

**José Teunissen**

José Teunissen is Professor of Fashion Theory at ArtEZ Institute of the Arts and Visiting Professor at the University of the Arts, London, as well as working as a freelance fashion curator. Her publications include: *Global Fashion, Local Tradition* (Terra, 2005), *Mode in Nederland* (Terra, 2006), *The Power of Fashion* (Terra 2006), and *Fashion & Imagination* (d'Jonge Hond, 2009).
j.teunissen@artez.nl

**Abstract**

During the 1990s, both Belgium and the Netherlands built up a name in the international fashion world. This article, which takes the Belgian success as its starting point to explore the less-known Dutch case, discusses what is meant by Dutch and Belgian fashion. A comparison of the history of fashion and clothing culture of the two countries—which border each other and in places speak the same language—reveals many similarities. For a long time both countries were influenced by Paris fashion. The proximity to Paris connected the Belgian clothing and textile industry to French couture, whereas the Netherlands was more reticent. Historically the Netherlands has had its own style with regard to clothing since the seventeenth century, and in the nineteenth century, this resulted in a flourishing culture of regional clothing, which is still worn in some parts of the Netherlands. In the 1980s, the Belgian government took its first initiatives to support young fashion talent. In 1988 this was followed by similar support on the part of the Dutch government. But whereas Belgium supported fashion designers through financial incentives for the textile and clothing industry, the Netherlands made fashion designers eligible for "art grants." The different approaches of the two countries in the 1980s had an influence on the outcome. On the one hand the Belgian designers were commercially more successful and became known worldwide in the field of fashion, while the Dutch were left behind. On the other hand they can also be related to the different background and fashion culture at the time. From different historical and industrial backgrounds the Belgian and the Dutch fashion cultures build up different concepts of "national identity" in fashion.

KEYWORDS: Belgium, The Netherlands, fashion design, identity, deconstruction, modernism, regional dress

At first sight it seems obvious that the two neighboring countries on the northwestern coast of the European continent would share a contemporary fashion culture: they have shared a long history, and were, for a short period in the nineteenth century, one country. However, a closer look reveals that there are as many differences as similarities.

In the 1980s, the Belgian government took its first initiatives to promote young fashion talents through "the Textile Plan," which enabled six young designers to start their own labels. They included Walter van Beirendonck, who had graduated from the fashion department of the Koninklijke Acadamie voor Schone Kunsten in Antwerp in 1980, followed by Dries van Noten, Dirk van Saene, Dirk Bikkembergs, Ann Demeulemeester, and Marina Yee, who completed their courses a year later in 1981. In the following years they visited Japan twice as a part of an economical mission and in 1986 they started presenting their collections twice a year at London Fashion Week. Their breakthrough came when they held their first group show in Westway Film Studio in London in 1988: the international press and buyers labeled them the "Antwerp Six." Talent scout and press agent Marysia Woroniecka described them as following: "What makes them special is that they are so fresh. Belgium had no tradition or history in fashion and that is why they are so original and open minded" (Es *et al.* 1989). This image has followed the Belgian designers, including the second generation that emerged in the 1990s, including Martin Margiela, A.F. Vandevorst, Veronique Branquinho, Haider Ackermann, and Raf Simons. They are renowned as skillful and creative avant-garde designers who happen to come from Belgium. The deconstructionist style that was seen to tie them together is notable for its avoidance of direct cultural references, but it captured a global trend at the time.

In 1988, the Dutch government also decided to support its fashion designers. But whereas Belgium supported fashion designers through financial incentives for the struggling textile and clothing industry, the Netherlands allowed fashion designers to apply for arts grants. When Viktor & Rolf (as part of Le Cri Néerlandais) and Orson & Bodil (by Alexander van Slobbe) began to show their collections in Paris in 1994, the Netherlands also began to play a role of some consequence in the world of international fashion. Their style was dubbed "Dutch Modernism," based on a conceptual approach and the development of clear forms. The international fashion press celebrated Le Cri Néerlandais (Viktor & Rolf, Saskia van Drimmelen, Lucas Ossendrijver, Pascale Gatzen, and Marcel Verheijen) and van Slobbe as the new identifiable fashion which, following the Japanese and the Belgians, was launching a new style and view on fashion and clothing in Paris, inspired by their specific national character. During the 1990s more young designers such as Klavers van Engelen and Spijkers & Spijkers started to build up an international label referring to their cultural roots. From the start in the early 1990s the fashion designers began to relate their designs to the strong Dutch modernistic and conceptual design tradition in graphic design, architecture, and interior design. "The Netherlands likes to think of itself as a modernist culture in which dry, minimalist and conceptual design is a focal point of modern idealism" (Huygen 2007).

In hindsight, the two neighboring countries' different approaches to supporting the emerging designer fashion sector are telling. The Belgian designers, backed by industry support, aimed for commercial success through brand building, whereas the Dutch, funded by art grants, adopted a probing experimental approach, which has just as often been directed at the art world as at fashion markets. The decisions to support fashion design in such different ways resulted from different industrial and cultural backgrounds at the time. At the same time, they marked out different trajectories for Belgian and Dutch fashion designers, which will be explored in this article which takes the Belgian success as its starting point to explore the less-known Dutch case. Unlike their Belgian counterparts, the Dutch fashion designers have increasingly turned to the cultural traditions and arts of the Netherlands, including regional dress, the Calvinists style of the seventeenth century, and craft traditions, in order to sustain and develop a distinctively Dutch designer fashion. The central argument of this article is that from different historical and industrial backgrounds the Belgians and the Dutch have constructed different concepts of "national identity" in fashion.

## National Identity: A Confection of Selective Memories

Since fashion works as a polycentric global system it is striking that designers and industries in small nations have taken part in a national debate since the 1980s. Throughout the world, we have seen a revival of interest in local heritage and craftsmanship in the past few years, and this has also applied to fashion. "National identity may be conceived as a confection of selective memories, generating traditions and rituals in order to reinforce ideas of permanence and longevity and also supplying the plebeian masses with a collection of codified emblems through which to foster national belonging and a sense of identification," explains Alison Goodrum in *The National Fabric*, illustrating how Paul Smith and Mulberry spread a British style throughout the world as a form of cultural imperialism of taste (Goodrum 2005: 62). Defining Britishness is relatively easy, since the English have played an important role in fashion history, especially in men's fashion. Savile Row and Carnaby Street both have a rich iconographic heritage that can be reused. The traditional male fashion and London street culture of the 1960s are recognized worldwide and have determined English taste and style (Breward *et al.* 2002).

But neither Belgium nor the Netherlands played such an influential role in the history of fashion. Therefore, in as far as they have wanted to market their national identity, identifying a "selective confection of memories" that can be turned into a piece of iconographic heritage has been a difficult task; one that Belgian and Dutch designers have approached very differently since the 1980s when talented young designers in the two countries succeeded in building up international reputations.

Jennifer Craik has tried to unravel a "national identity" in the dressing style of Australia, also a country with no history in fashion. According to her a national sense of style or fashion it the expressive encapsulation of the cultural psyche or *zeitgeist* of a place or country through its people (Craik 2009: 413). The spirit of nationalism exists when three realms come together, aesthetic distinctiveness, cultural practice, and cultural articulation. By the latter she means the ability to project style to a point that is taken to be accepted as the "natural" identity of a nation. Within this framework we can consider the reticent attitude of the Dutch towards Paris fashion and the soberness in style of the Dutch woman as a typical cultural articulation of the Dutch nation.

The success of Belgian Fashion, on the other hand, seemed primarily an outcome of the Textile Plan and its subsequent identification with the city of Antwerp, where political and economic circumstances functioned as catalysts for the identification of a creative practice according to Javier Gimeno Martinez in his study on the "Antwerp Six." He does not believe in impositions of national boundaries on notions of style nowadays in a world where communication and media are eroding national boundaries (Gimeno Martinez 2008: 52).

## The Story behind Belgian Fashion: Changing National Politics

In 1981 the Belgian government launched the Textile Plan (Het Textiel Plan), an ambitious plan to revitalize the failing textile industry. The new Institute for Textile and Clothing of Belgium (ITCB) started with an overall budget of 687 million euros, divided into three parts. First, there was a financial component of 496 million euros for innovations and the reorganization of companies. Then there was a service component of 141 million euros for marketing and education, mainly used for large promotional campaigns. In 1983 "Dit is België," which was launched by the ITCB, enhanced the image of Belgian fashion. It also meant the start of the Golden Spoel (Golden Bobbin) Award in 1983, a prize that gave young designers the opportunity to finance a collection. Thanks to this prize they also came into contact with the local manufacturers and producers in Belgian industry. Finally, there was a third social component of 50 million euros to alleviate unavoidable lay-offs. As a result of both the prize and the promotional campaign the young designers of the "Antwerp Six" gained access to production facilities and they were able to attract a lot of attention internationally. In this way they could slowly build up their own companies (Moons 2008: 70).

In the 1990s it became clear that the cooperation between the young designers and the Belgian manufacturers was not working out very well. Therefore, designers such as Ann Demeulemeester and Dirk Bikkembergs were forced to search for producers outside Belgium. In the end the majority of Belgian manufacturers and producers did not survive: they could not compete with outsourcing. In retrospect, the service component turned out to be the only successful part of the Textile Plan. The research and development measures, as well as the stimulating and coordinating role of the ITCB with regard to training, education, management, and networking, were particularly seen as being responsible for a new dynamic approach in the sector. In 2008 this resulted in twenty-three independent designers and thirty-five companies engaged in the fashion business full-time in Flanders and Brussels (Moons 2008: 75). As a result of federalization in 1993 the service component was split into a Flemish and a Walloon part. In 1998 it was succeeded by the Flanders Fashion Institute (FFI), an initiative of the Flemish government. On the one hand, the FFI stimulates the entrepreneurship of the Flemish fashion industry by providing business training; on the other hand, it helps to promote Flemish designers in Belgium and abroad. And although the Flemish promotion is strong, they have not succeeded in changing the brand Belgian designers into Flemish or Antwerp designers. The legitimacy crisis of the Belgian nation in the early 2000s shows that co-branding with the nation can also have a negative effect.

Gradually the term Belgian Fashion was geographically reduced to Antwerp Fashion (Gimeno Martinez 2008: 64). They soon developed an infrastructure, with the MoMu Antwerp (2002) and Flanders Fashion Institute (FFI) helping promote Flemish design abroad. Political circumstances in general and federalization played an important role in modifying the meaning of Belgian Fashion.

In this way the promotional institutions were not silent actors but defining agents in the creation of the concept of Belgian/Antwerp Fashion. The label "Belgian Fashion" therefore can be seen as an outcome of the Textile Plan of the 1980s in a process where political and economic circumstances acted as catalysts for the identification of a creative practice with a concept of place (Gimeno Martinez 2008: 64).

Francesca Granata (2008) has recently argued that Belgian or Belgian-trained designers have a remarkable interest in the carnivalesque, seen as a set of practices based on inversions and travesties, as well as carnival iconography. She describes Bernhard Willhelm, Walter van Beirendonck, and Martin Margiela as examples of the carnivalesque and pursues a comparison with the fashion house Norine and their relation with Margritte. However, most contemporary Belgian designers do not fit this "aesthetic dimension" of the carnivalesque.

## The Dutch Way to Success: Funding and Subsidies for Design Concepts

Fashion in the Netherlands became much more sophisticated in the 1980s. New developments in Paris were followed with interest. The Japanese designers Yohji Yamamoto and Comme des Garçons made an impression in the Netherlands with conceptual designs in which they investigated the form and meaning of clothing. New stores appeared in the Netherlands specializing in these designer clothes (Teunissen 2006). Dutch fashion students also showed an interest, identifying with the ideas and well-thought-out concepts that the Japanese employed in their designs. They also felt deeply inspired by the "Antwerp Six" and their deconstructionist approach and especially their courage to present themselves as young and independent designers among the top designers of London and Paris. They did not get the same fundamental support from the government but they could rely on the newly established "art grant" from The Fund for Visual Art, Design and Architecture (BKVB).

This organization was established in 1988 to support the careers of talented graduate artists and designers with an incentive subsidy. This sum of money supported them for a year and enabled them to buy materials. The BKVB fund started with an overall budget of 23 million euros for 1988 and 1989. Fashion designers received around 700,000 euro. Compared to Belgium's Textile Plan investment in 1981 that delivered 141 million euros for marketing and education in Fashion, this was just a small amount of money. In 1990, a number of small labels were established in this way and managed to build up an international reputation and clientele following a joint presentation in London, similar to the "Antwerp Six" before them. They called themselves the GILL group (an amalgamation of Gletcher, Lawina, and Illustrious Imps and the shoe label Lola Pagola) and had their collections photographed by the then young photographer Inez van Lamsweerde. However, none of them succeeded in making their designer labels commercially viable in the long term. The main reason was that they were not supported by any investors and it was difficult to find small-scale production facilities. In 1991 the fund shut off the supply of government subsidies, as it considered that fashion brands should be able to stand on their own feet and the funding was meant to be only temporary.

In 1994 Le Cri Néerlandais and Orson & Bodil, the second generation of designers funded by BKVB, held their first show in Paris. The designer Alexander van Slobbe had started Orson & Bodil in 1988 together with Nanet van der Kleijn. Both had worked for labels in the Dutch clothing industry that had already been outsourced since the early 1970s. Van der Kleijn and van Slobbe were not happy with the cheap and simple clothing this system produced. As a reaction they developed their label Orson & Bodil dedicated to handicraft and conceptual design driven by an intrinsic love for clothing, form, material, and workmanship. In the first years they earned their money with freelance commissions for the industry while the grants of BKVB enabled them to develop Orson & Bodil as entrepreneurs. The designers of Le Cri Néerlandais on the other hand had graduated at ArtEZ Institute of the Arts in 1992. With BKVB funding, they had received a grant that enabled them to develop a first collection. They decided to present their collection, that they could hardly produce, in Paris as "The New Dutch Six" following the "Antwerp Six." It was an instant media success. The international press labeled them instantly "Dutch modernists" (van den Berg 2008: 102). They saw themselves as exponents of a strong Dutch design tradition that established a reputation in the twentieth century with austere, clear-cut modernistic design, in the field of graphic design and architecture. In press coverage and exhibitions that followed they were associated with "Droog Design"—the famous Dutch product design foundation—which had also appeared on the international scene in the early 1990s (Teunissen and van Zijl 2000). Different from the Belgian fashion designers that were building up their reputation mainly by marketing and developing business, the Dutch designers presented themselves primarily as artist/designers derived from the modernistic design heritage of the Netherlands.

From the beginning of their career in 1994 until 2000 Viktor & Rolf made only artistic presentations without having a wearable collection to sell. Lacking the money to build up a professional fashion business they preferred to concentrate on presenting concepts and ideas on fashion with grants from the BKVB fund. Only in 2000 when a Japanese investor gave them the opportunity did they start their commercial label. In 1993 Alexander van Slobbe was invited by the investor van Veldhoven to start a menswear collection, So, which became very successful label on the Japanese market. However van Slobbe was forced to cease his womenswear collection Orson & Bodil in 1995 because he did not find a financial backer. Therefore the decision was taken to focus solely on So's menswear.

## What Went Before? A Short History of the Belgian and the Dutch Fashion Industry

Until the 1960s French *haute couture* was leading and dominant in European fashion (Lipovetsky 1994). While Belgium was a close follower of French fashion, the Dutch already had a more restrained attitude towards Paris fashion. In the early twentieth century Belgium developed a strong textile and garment industry of its own, and was an important importer of French fashions. The Belgian producers were often privileged compared to their French counterparts. Not only were they located closer to Paris than many French manufacturers, they could also buy official couture licenses, as Belgium was a foreign country (Pouillard 2008: 9). In 1919 Belgium initiated a *Chambre Syndicale de la Haute Couture Belge* that worked in close cooperation with the French *Chambre Syndicale de la Haute Couture,* dedicated to crafting and selling authorized copies from Paris. This enabled Belgium to expand its entire textile and garment industry (Pouillard 2008).

From 1916 to 1952 the Norine house in Brussels was the only fashion house that created its own designs instead of copying Paris. Norine was run by the couple Paul-Gustave van Hecke and Honorine (Norine) Deschrijver, who had more artistic ambitions. Like Paul Poiret and Coco Chanel, they practiced couture as art by incorporating an avant-garde attitude in their creations and by cooperating closely with artists. In their case they hired the artist René Magritte to make adverts and fashion paintings. In addition, they implemented a modern, graphic style in Norine, integrating Surrealist imaginary into fashion (Bernheim 2008: 17).

Until the 1960s the Dutch were also strict followers of French fashion, but both the inexpensive, ready-made garment industry as well as the *haute couture* were always simplified and made more practical, to suit to Dutch taste (Teunissen 2006). In 1928 Joan Praetorius was the first Dutch couturier to establish a fashion house in his own name. His debut show was favorably reviewed in the press, with praise for the international appeal, as well as appreciation of his personal style. Rather than adopting the Parisian *garçonne* style, Praetorius was more into fuller figures, emphasizing women's curves with loose flowing lines. This latter aspect was particularly appreciated by both Dutch press and the consumers, as it suited Dutch women better (Teunissen 2006: 172).

It was not until after World War II that new Dutch designers emerged. This new generation, represented by Max Heijmans and Dick Holthuis, closely followed Parisian fashions. They often worked with patterns purchased at the shows of Coco Chanel—and later Christian Dior—which they were licensed to copy. In these years Dutch couturiers translated French fashions to suit Dutch taste. In practice, this meant that they simplified the styles and made them more sober. When they visited Paris, they took patterns for practical designs home with them and left behind the more frivolous creations.

During the first half of the twentieth century the Netherlands and Belgium had a fairly comparable fashion system and fashion culture. They were both close followers of Paris fashions. However, due to their proximity, the Belgian manufacturers were more closely connected to the couture practice of Paris. Furthermore, both countries had their own avant-garde exceptions. Nevertheless, the Dutch were more restrained followers of the Paris fashion style. The Belgian consumers only made small and practical modifications to French fashion design—i.e. darker shades and heavier fabrics that suited the Belgian climate better (Pouillard 2008: 8). The Dutch were also practical followers of the French fashion examples, but the ready-made garment industry was reluctant to adopt Paris fashion. Magazines and newspapers continually expressed many reservations about the frivolity of French fashion by presenting "a practical, no-nonsense" Dutch woman as the cultural opposite of the "elegant, fashionable, fashion consuming" Parisienne (Teunissen 1990).

## Fashion Culture of Belgium and the Netherlands in the Twenty-first Century

In 2008 the whole textile industry in the Netherlands reached a turnover of 8 billion euros. This turnover includes all textile industries, including those that manufacture curtains and bed linen. In the same year, Belgium achieved a total turnover of 4 billion euros. Both countries have a small group of well-known designers with a reputation in the international fashion world. In the Netherlands, Viktor & Rolf, Alexander van Slobbe, Spijkers & Spijkers, Francisco van Benthum, and People of the Labyrinth amongst others are on this list. In addition, there are a number of designers who present themselves on the national and international scene, though most do not have a collection that is sold. In 2008, Belgium had twenty-three designer labels with regular catwalk shows, including Ann Demeulemeester, Dries van Noten, Haider Ackermann, and Walter van Beirendonck. In 2009, this number was slightly reduced as a result of the financial crisis and, for example, Veronique Branquinho went bankrupt. Compared to Belgium the number of entrepreneurial leading designers in the Netherlands is smaller, but the commercial trade and the number of large commercial fashion brands is larger. The Netherlands has some popular middle-market to premium brands that do well, such as G-Star, Mexx, Turnover, Stills, and Oilily. They have built up a successful ready-to-wear industry with labels as Stills, Turnover, and Sandwich providing the Scandinavian and German market with fashionable clothes for the practical, casually dressed Nordic woman.

In the 1960s the Netherlands was one of the first countries to move textile and clothing production to Portugal and the Far East. As a supplier to Paris and also due to a very successful Fordist system, Belgium retained its textile industry up to the end of the twentieth century.

The Belgian designers still use Paris as the platform for their presentations and sales. One significant factor in this development has been the hundreds of fashion weeks that have appeared on the scene in the last fifteen years that are primarily oriented towards promoting the designers' own country, their own culture, by means of "the local fashion" visible by using local crafts (Teunissen 2005: 9–18). It is remarkable that Antwerp did not start a fashion week: the designers still use Paris as the platform for their presentations and sales. Located one hour from Paris, Belgium does not need a fashion week to promote their national design. They have proven that strategies other than highlighting the "local heritage" can be successful. At the end of the 1990s the city of Antwerp was transformed into a fashion hotspot thanks to the efforts of Linda Loppa, director of the fashion department of the Antwerp school and Geert Brulot (who as a boutique owner was involved in actively promoting the "Antwerp Six"). They were both important in the realization of the fashion museum (MoMu) in 2002 focusing primarily on Belgian fashion. The museum, located in the ModeNatie (Fashion Nation) building, also houses the famous fashion department of the Koninklijke Academie voor de Kunsten. The Flanders Fashion Institute (FFI), which stimulates enterprise in the fashion industry in Flanders and promotes it nationally and internationally, is also located there. In addition, the designers Dries van Noten, Ann Demeulemeester, and Walter van Beirendonck have their flagship stores nearby. This means that Antwerp is a dynamic fashion city that attracts many tourists every year. In this way Antwerp has put Belgium on the map as a fashion country.

Fashion culture in the Netherlands has developed differently in the last decades. There has been a fashion week in Amsterdam since 2004 (Amsterdam International Fashion Week, AIFW), where young Dutch talent is presented. The more established designers such as Viktor & Rolf, Francisco van Benthum, and Spijkers & Spijkers continue to present their shows outside the Netherlands. This means that the AIFW is above all a platform for young talented designers and not a place where buyers and trade fairs purchase collections. In 2008, the Red Light Fashion Amsterdam project also started in Amsterdam, where young designers were offered a former brothel to use as a studio. In 2009, sixteen designers became established there, using the space mainly as a place to work and for presentations. Only the odd designer actually sells anything there. This place has attracted and still attracts a great deal of international fashion interest, and the intention is to help the designers here with professionalizing their business.

In addition to Amsterdam, the city of Arnhem is also very active. In 2005, a fashion biennale was established in cooperation with the Institute of the Arts ArtEZ fashion department, which exhibits fashion as a cultural phenomenon. In 2007, the city council also set up the project 100% Mode where young designers can rent cheap studios and shops in the Klarendal district. In contrast with the Red Light Fashion Initiative, designers are only eligible for this sort of space if their business plan is in order and they actually open a shop. Arnhem has also strengthened its fashion infrastructure by opening a sample studio where designers starting up can carry out small productions close to home.

Whereas Antwerp has been successfully transformed into a commercial and fashion tourism hotspot, the Dutch still maintain their focus on presenting interesting designs and the concept of Dutch designers. The Red Light Fashion Amsterdam and the Fashion Biennale Arnhem, which explores fashion emphatically as a cultural phenomenon, exemplify this clearly. It appears that the Dutch designers since the 1990s have gone even further in their engagement with cultural heritage. In particular, they have engaged with two elements in Dutch history—regional dress and the bourgeois fashions of the seventeenth century.

## Dutch Fashion and Regional Dress

Since the beginning of the new millennium Dutch fashion designers have shown an interest in folklore, regional dress, and the related local crafts and methods that are used. This is remarkable, considering their image of modernity and conceptual design. In 2001, van Slobbe started to use horizontal folds, amongst other techniques, for his *Re-wind* menswear collection (Figure 1).

This principle was used in the Province of Zeeland to fold clothes up as compactly as possible so that they could be easily transported in the case of flooding. In his own collection of menswear entitled *Hope* (2008), Francisco van Benthum also plays with traditional elements of local costume, such as the use of buttons, pom-poms, and old-fashioned baggy trousers. And in their collection entitled *Fashion Show* (Fall/Winter 2007/8) Viktor & Rolf applied dots and spots as traditionally used in the village of Staphorst, with traditional red coral, Zeeland buttons, and various folding techniques employed in traditional costume.

In these cases, it was not the aim of the designers to evoke a romantic picture of bygone times. They used form and technique purely as an inspiration to achieve a lucid, modern design. Seen in this light, how is it

**Figure 1**
Jacket made of farmers' handkerchiefs torn into strips. So by Alexander van Slobbe, *Re-wind* collection, 2001. Image courtesy of Alexander van Slobbe/Orson & Bodil. Photograph: Dan Lecca.

possible that the modernistic, progressive Dutch fashion mentality is also being devoted to tradition and regional costume? The first explanation lies in the fact that the Netherlands has hardly ever played a role in the official fashion history, although it does have a striking culture of traditional costume. If there is such a thing as a clothing tradition in the Netherlands, it is centered on regional dress. In places such as Urk, Marken, and Spakenburg, regional dress is still worn, albeit to a limited degree and only by a hard core of devotees. In addition, it is exploited to the full for tourism purposes. Every Dutch person is familiar with the culture of clogs, windmills, and Delftware, but hardly anyone knows that, in contrast to many other countries, the Dutch explicitly cultivated regional dress in the nineteenth century to escape from modernization, urbanization, consumerism, and other urban whims (de Jong 1998: 67–82).

Johan Le Francq van Berkheij noticed in the first ethnographic study about the Netherlands, *Natuurlijke historie van Holland* (1776 vol III, p711 cit: Koolhaas-Grosfeld: 2010*)*, that the true Dutchman was honest, sincere, and did not like any pretense or show. The big *diversity* in regional dress (each village and province had its own style) was, according to Le Francq van Berkheij, a characteristic of the national identity of Holland.

Dutch sociologists and ethnologists claim that regional dress fulfilled an important function in the realization of the political ideals of the country in this period. In the early nineteenth century, the Netherlands had again become an assorted collection of provinces, just as in the seventeenth century (de Jong 1998: 67–82). In 1830, when the Netherlands suddenly acquired the name the Kingdom of the Netherlands, after the secession of Belgium, it was the monarchy and traditional custom that were responsible for providing the necessary unity. The provinces were allowed to cultivate their own origins, cultures, and traditions as long as everyone was prepared to fall in line with the national government. The publisher Evert Maaskamp started in 1803 with his Dutch regional costume books *Afbeeldingen van kleeding, zeden en gewoonten in de Bataafsche Republiek, met den aanvang van den negentiende eeuw*, where ethnic variety/diversity of the provinces was defined as a crucial element of the Dutch identity (Koolhaas-Grosfeld 2010: 163; Figure 2). According to the historian Herman Pleij, this also can be explained by the fact that since the late Middle Ages, the Dutch have had a culture primarily based on solidarity rather than on nationalism (Pleij 1991).

What deterred the Dutch from participating in upcoming French fashion in the nineteenth century was the fact that they saw it as the result of an anonymous urban culture, while most people in the Netherlands lived in villages or small towns. They were afraid they would lose their own identity and culture to city fashions and the new nation, and that is why they preferred their traditional rural life, which they regarded as being pure and intact (Rooijakkers 1998: 175). Thus, to a certain extent, they sought dress forms and decorations through which they could express creativity and taste, away from the fashions of the day.

What did and does regional dress offer the Dutch that cosmopolitan fashion cannot? Regional costume is generally regarded as a style that is not subject to change, in contrast to fashion. Regional costume is based on fixed codes and significances in clothing: it shows the social status of people, which religion they embrace, and their civil status, by the colors, ribbons or buttons they display. In short, it is a dress system that offers society various guidelines, certainties, and solidarity.

By contrast, fashion is a self-reflecting system: it constantly changes in form and meaning, and primarily refers to itself—just like autonomous art (Barthes 1967; Calefato, in Teunissen and Brand 2006: 126–52). To become familiar with the ever-changing fashion codes, you have to move in the right circles and know the rules. This basic principle

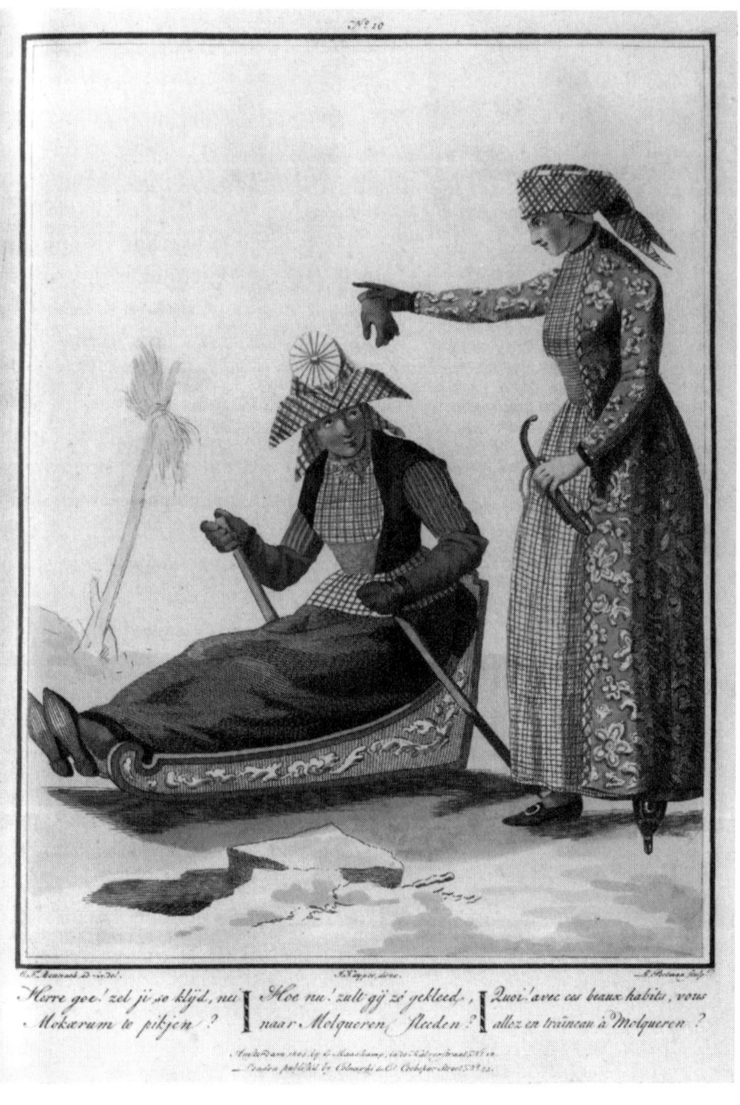


**Figure 2**
Woman and girl from West Friesland. The drawing is a reproduction of figure 10 from the book *Afbeeldingen van kleding, zeden en gewoonten*, 1804. Image courtesy of Library University of Amsterdam, Special Collections.

of fashion explains why there are so many fashion magazines. For example, each target group has its own magazine that shows what may be worn at any particular moment. Finally, fashion and regional dress identify people in different ways—fashion mostly through class; regional dress, mostly through origin or birthplace. In a sense this makes fashion more democratic than regional dress. Fashion, in the end is accessible to everyone, as long as he or she has enough money. There are no dress restrictions for the different social classes, whereas social restrictions do apply for regional costume. Fashion offers the wearer the opportunity to fit in with the group, but also creates scope to emphasize one's own individuality: you can adopt a distinctive look. In this sense fashion was ideal for meeting the needs of the modern citizens who arose as a result of the Enlightenment and democracy in the nineteenth century: citizens who wished to belong to a group by means of the way they dress, and who at the same time expressed themselves in clothing as individuals within that group (Simmel 1919; Lipovetsky 1994).

By contrast, in Dutch regional dress there are strict social rules: people had to dress according to their social standing, profession, and civil status. Nevertheless, there was some leeway for individual variation. People could give the waistcoat, shawl or other parts of the costume a unique and personal look with handmade work, embroidery, and variations in fabric. It was often a question of who could make the most attractive waistcoat, and then others would follow this: therefore the Dutch regional dress culture developed an extensive culture of handmade work and treating textiles in which individual creativity was expressed. One striking element in many traditional costumes is the use of colorful (chintz) fabrics that were incorporated into Dutch dress culture from India via the Dutch East India Company. In the seventeenth century, rich ladies began to wear chintz jackets as domestic clothing, and later people began to use these fabrics to decorate traditional costumes. Antique chintz was often incorporated in the most beautiful clothes, the so-called "spruced-up" clothes.

Accordingly, regional dress became the "romantic" symbol of the preservation and protection of one's own culture and traditions while, paradoxically, it also demonstrated, with the use of chintz, that the Netherlands was a worldly nation where people were open to influences from outside. Fashion from Paris was viewed with distrust, but beautiful textiles from the Orient could easily be incorporated in a traditional outfit. People were certainly open-minded, but did not like the superficial ostentation of metropolitan fashion.

Following the theory of Jennifer Craik we can conclude that the Dutch have a distinctive clothing style or preference: an "aesthetic distinctiveness" and "cultural practice" that is based on certain techniques in folding and pleating, the use of chintz, and—as I will discuss below—the soberness, for instance, expressed in the seventeenth century black-and-white clothing. Contemporary Dutch designers regard the traditional crafts and manual techniques, as discussed earlier, as a rich source of inspiration that they can use to develop new and fresh designs but that at the same time exude an atmosphere of traditional quality and lend "identity" to a product.

The fact that fashion designer van Slobbe fires ceramic pearls in the spirit of Vermeer (in conjunction with Royal Tichelaar Makkum, the oldest porcelain factory in the Netherlands) is an excellent example of this. The pearls acquire an extra dimension with the reference to Dutch history and to *The Girl with a Pearl Earring* by Vermeer. Moreover, the love of fine craftsmanship is clearly expressed, making it a valuable artistic object. Along the same lines, Viktor & Rolf also regularly take their own heritage as a starting point. Viktor & Rolf studied Dutch lace for their *Bedtime Story* collection (2005/6) and based *Silver* (2006/7) on the traditional Dutch custom of silver-plating baby shoes. The duo even based the *Fashion Show* collection (Fall/Winter 2007/8) on various styles of traditional dress. In addition to regional dress, this collection also covers the fashion show as a social phenomenon. Each model wore a readymade installation of sound and light, where the installation itself again influenced the design.

Where regional dress is built on (relatively) *fixed meanings* and codes indicating the *social position* and geographical *place* of the wearer, fashion only seems to indicate a *temporal* dimension. Seen in this way, fashion and the "national identity" appear to be irreconcilable, but comparing the streetscape of Amsterdam, the available brands, the discourse of designers and fashion magazines to that of Paris it has to be acknowledged that there are different clothing and fashion cultures in the two cities. Especially in the imagination of the fashionable woman there is a remarkable difference. According to Agnes Rocamora, la Parisienne is as much an imagined as a living reality (Rocamora 2009: 90). For over a century in literature, art, and fashion magazines she has been the person who sets trends and give the clothes she wears "the consecration of taste, the baptism of fashion" (Martin-Chauffier 2007: 35; Rocamora 2009). She was the elegant and tasteful woman (Steele 1988: 76–7), whereas the Dutch woman since 1900 in all Dutch fashion magazines was described as the "practical' woman" opposed to "la Parisienne" (Teunissen 1990).

The way in which the popular magazine *Margriet* (founded in 1938) reported on the Parisian showed, for example, how reserved the attitudes were as regards the latest fashions. Even as late as 1960, the magazine stated that the creations shown in Paris "are not to be worn by ordinary mortals or are of an exceptional, profligate luxuriousness" (Teunissen 1990: 90). Paris stood for extravagance, the opposite of virtues such as respectability and thrift, which were highly regarded by Dutch readers. The magazine tried to discourage any of its readers who might have fashionable pretensions by continually comparing the "elegant" Parisienne and the Dutch woman who is nothing of the sort:

> There is simply nothing that can be done about it. We Dutch women have a tendency to become fat. Apparently we eat too well and are too fond of the coziness surrounding the teapot and the cookie tin. What may be pretty on a delicate French girl was not necessarily attractive on a strapping Dutch girl. After all, nature had made her one size larger. (Teunissen 1990: 90)

Besides a distinctive aesthetic dimension Dutch fashion and clothing style also possesses the "cultural articulation" (Craik 2009: 413) or "cultural attitude" of solidarity, open-mindedness, and a recurrent reticence about French fashion. This had already started in the seventeenth century.

## Dutch Fashion and the Golden Age

Only the typical Dutch dress of the Golden Age is acknowledged in the history books as being any kind of noteworthy fashion: in fact, it is the only moment at which the Netherlands appears in fashion history at all: this probably refers back to the one period when the Netherlands was a world power and recognized style arbiter. While dignitaries at the French and English courts switched to colorful and extravagant clothing, the Dutch regents continued to dress in austere black garments, decorated with white lace and starched collars (Laver 1985: 108). In this way they underlined the strict Calvinist attitude to life and also made it clear that, in contrast to France with its court culture, the Netherlands was an egalitarian and more or less democratic country. In his book *An Embarrassment of Riches,* Simon Schama refers to this as a typically Dutch solution to an uneasy and ambiguous relationship between the Protestant regents and their newly acquired wealth and power (Schama 1987). If we look beyond the surface of the seventeenth-century Dutch clothes themselves, we see that little has changed in terms of Dutch attitudes toward dress and fashion. The Dutch did not delight in ostentation and social display even then. People preferred a sober, refined, black outfit, not only to give subtle expression to their own tastes, but also to illustrate civil ideals of equality.

The fact that modernism found such a fertile breeding ground in the Netherlands about three centuries later is related to this same mentality. In modernistic design concepts and ideology are also of essential importance: a good design should be protected against superfluous decoration and ornamentation. Form arises from ideas. This attitude to design is visible in the work of all Dutch designers. Even the work of Viktor & Rolf, which is occasionally experienced as being baroque, can always be reduced to a single central idea. For example, the entire *Flowerbomb* collection (2005), which appears to be rather exuberant, is based entirely on the principle of the bow (Figure 3).

As regards traditional regional dress, it could be said that this style of dress was also based on a culture of mutual solidarity, just like the fashions of the seventeenth century. The Netherlands has never been afraid to assume its own idiosyncratic attitude in fashion. Founded on a clear, characteristic vision of culture and ideals, a characteristic notion of dress and fashion, "a cultural articulation," also arose at a relatively early stage during the seventeenth century.

**Figure 3**
Viktor & Rolf, *Flowerbomb* collection, Spring/Summer 2005. The whole collection is based on the idea of a bow and the dress is made from one elaborate bow. Image courtesy of Peter Stigter (photographer).

## Conclusion

From a relatively comparable history the two neighboring countries, Belgium and the Netherlands, developed in the 1980s very different concepts of "national identity" as a strategy to promote their fashion designers. Where Alison Goodrum (2005) describes "national identity" in British fashion as "a confection of selective memories" being recognizable for both the local inhabitants as well as an international consumer market, this was only true for the Dutch designers. In promoting So by Alexander van Slobbe in Japan during the 1990s, the Japanese kept emphasizing the importance of enhancing the products' Dutch identity. Lacking the clear British iconography of Paul Smith, So by Alexander van Slobbe managed to convince the Japanese market with press material telling the story of the long history of the Dutch in abstract, modernistic, formal design (van den Berg 2008).

The Belgian designers were also successful in Japan but none of them referred to their Belgian design roots. Internationally they were seen as "creative" and "original" designers having managed to transform Belgium and Antwerp into a fashion hotspot based on an ingenious government-driven marketing and business strategy for young Belgian designers followed by a convincing city branding of Antwerp by the Flanders federal government. The Dutch search for a cultural identity can partly be explained as a compensation for the lack of an industry network. But, as stated in this article, Dutch Modernism in fashion can also be seen as an integral part of a strong and vivid Dutch design tradition and mentality.

## Acknowledgments

I would like to thank the NWO-research team *Dutch Identity in a Globalised World* (Prof Dr Anneke Smelik, Prof Dr Dany Jacobs, Prof Dr Michiel Scheffer, Maaike Feitsma, Anja Köppchen, Constantin von Maltzahn).

## References

Barthes, Roland. 1967. *Système de la Mode.* Paris: De Seuil.

Bernheim, Nele. 2008. "Maison Norine, Brussels: Belgian Avant-garde Couture, *c.* 1916–1952." In Nele Bernheim (ed.) *Symposium 1: Modus Operandi*, pp. 17–35. Antwerp: MoMu.

Breward, Christopher, B. Conekin and C. Cox (eds). 2002. *The Englishness of English Dress.* Oxford: Berg.

Craik, Jennifer. 2009. "Is Australian Fashion and Dress Distinctively Australian?" *Fashion Theory* 13: 409–41.

de Jong, Ad. 1998. "Dracht en eendracht. De politieke dimensie van klederdrachten, 1850–1920." In Dolly Verhoeven (ed.) *Klederdracht en kleedgedrag. Het kostuum Harer Majesteits onderdanen, 1898–1998*, pp. 67–82. Nijmegen: SUN.

Es, Gerdi, A. Govaerts and Simone van Riel. 1989. *Belgie: Mode in de lage landen.* Antwerp: Cantecleer.

Gimeno Martinez, Javier. 2008. "Fashion, Country and City: The Fashion Industry and the Construction of Collective Identities (1981–2001)." In Nele Bernheim (ed.) *Symposium 1: Modus Operandi,* pp. 17–35. Antwerp: MoMu.

Goodrum, Alison. 2005. *The National Fabric: Fashion, Britishness, Globalisation*. Oxford: Berg.

Granata, Francesca. 2008. "Fashion of Inversion: The Carnivalesque and the Grotesque in Contemporary Belgian Fashion." In Nele Bernheim (ed.) *Symposium 1: Modus Operandi*, pp. 17–35. Antwerp: MoMu.

Huygen, Frederique. 2007. *Visies op Vormgeving*. Amsterdam: Architectura & Natura Pers.

Koolhaas-Grosfeld, Eveline. 2010. *De Ontdekking van de Nederlander. In boeken en prenten rond 1800*. Zuthpen: Walburg pers.

Laver, James. 1985. *Costume and Fashion*. London: Thames & Hudson.

Lipovetsky, Gilles. 1994. *The Empire of Fashion: Dressing Democracy*. Princeton, NJ: Princeton University Press.

Martin-Chauffier, Gilles. 2007. *Une vraie Parisienne*. Paris: Grasset.

Moons, A. 2008. "To Be (in) or Not Be (in): The Constituting Processes and Impact Indicators of the Flemish Designer Fashion Industry Undressed." In Nele Bernheim (ed.) *Symposium 1: Modus Operandi*, pp. 69–82. Antwerp: MoMu.

Pleij, Herman. 1991. *Het Nederlandse onbehagen*. Amsterdam: Prometheus.

Pouillard, Véronique. 2008. "Before Antwerp? Reproducing Fashions in Interwar Belgium." In Nele Bernheim (ed.) *Symposium 1: Modus Operandi*, pp. 1–15. Antwerp: MoMu.

Rocamora, Agnes. 2009. *Fashioning the City*. London: I.B. Taurus.

Rooijakkers, Gerard. 1998. "Dragers van traditie? Klederdracht als culturele constructive." In Dolly Verhoeven (ed.) *Klederdracht en kleedgedrag: Het kostuum Harer Majesteits onderdanen, 1898–1998*, pp. 173–89. Nijmegen: SUN.

Schama, Simon. 1987. *The Embarrassment of Riches: An Interpretation of Dutch Culture in the Golden Age*. New York: Knopff.

Simmel, Georg. 1919. "Die Mode." In *Philosophische kultur*. Leipzig: Alfred Kröner Verlag.

Steele, Valerie. 1988. *Paris Fashion*. New York: Oxford University Press.

Teunissen, José. 1990. "Margriet en Avenue als modemakers." In Pauline Terreehorst (ed.) *Modus*, pp. 88–92. Amsterdam: De Balie.

Teunissen, José. 2005. "On the Globalisation of Fashion." In José Teunissen (ed.) *Global Fashion, Local Tradition*, pp. 8–23. Arnhem: Terra.

Teunissen, José. 2006. *Mode in Nederland*. Arnhem: Terra.

Teunissen, José and Jan Brand (eds). 2006. *The Power of Fashion*. Arnhem: Terra.

Teunissen, José and Ida van Zijl. 2000. *Droog en Dutch Design*. Utrecht: Centraal Museum.

van den Berg, Nanda. 2008. *Alexander van Slobbe*. Arnhem: d'Jonge Hond & ArtEZ Press.

*Fashion Theory,* Volume 15, Issue 2, pp. 177–200
DOI: 10.2752/175174111X12954359478681
Reprints available directly from the Publishers.
Photocopying permitted by licence only.

# From Design Nations to Fashion Nations? Unpacking Contemporary Scandinavian Fashion Dreams[1]

**Marie Riegels Melchior**

Marie Riegels Melchior is a part-time lecturer at the Department of Ethnology, University of Copenhagen, and Research Fellow at The Danish Museum of Art & Design. In 2008 she did her PhD on Danish fashion in the period 1950–2008. Currently she is engaged in a study of fashion in museums.
frazerriegels@hotmail.com

## Abstract

To many people, the link between Scandinavia and design is still a familiar story of functionalism and the social democratic welfare states of the twentieth century. But until recently the Scandinavian countries—Denmark, Norway, and Sweden—had not sought to connect themselves with fashion design. This, however, has changed since the turn of the millennium. Present-day government institutions, industry organizations, fashion media, and industry form partnerships that not only give the fashion industry a prominent status in deindustrialized economies, but also potentially change the image of the nations. In this article

**I unfold what I term the fashion dreams of the Scandinavian countries in order to examine what their experiences tell us—on one hand, the role of fashion for the nation, and on the other hand, the contribution of national governments to the polycentrism of the fashion world.**

**KEYWORDS: Denmark, Norway, Sweden, fashion design, identity, industry policy**

From design nations to fashion nations? This is the trajectory that lies at heart of this article, and when looking at the Scandinavian countries in the course of recent history, it is a striking development. The dominant design movement of the Scandinavian countries arose in the 1950s and 1960s and still holds significance. But the new focus on fashion in Scandinavia raises the possibility of a great shift currently taking place within the Scandinavian countries, not only in terms of their culture and economy, but also with respect to the image they project to the world.

Since the mid-twentieth century, the social democratic welfare states of the Scandinavian countries have combined industrial production with high living standards and a high degree of social equality. Simultaneously, they have also earned international recognition for their socially embedded functionalist design, primarily of furniture but also of lamps, kitchenware, and textiles (Dickson 2006; Halén and Wickman 2003). "Scandinavian design," defined first and foremost in relation to British and US export markets, came to mean genuine design solutions for everyday life, designs that do not follow the prosaic flux of fashion, but rather pursue the good life as a nearly utopian ideal (Davies 2003). This image styled the Scandinavian countries as design nations, and continues to characterize Denmark, Norway, and Sweden, both locally and internationally. By design nation I mean when design not only stands for the act of innovation and giving form to material objects, but when it is also made subject to government strategies in order to pursue better solutions for the future of the nation. In the aftermath of the Second World War the Scandinavian countries can be regarded as design nations as their governments not only supported the boom of design consumption locally and internationally, but also believed in the egalitarian vision of the ability to design through modernist architecture and home interior design, the good life for all, which was the credo of the young social democratic welfare states.

However, after deindustrialization and the increasing political dismantling of the welfare states at the end of the twentieth century (Højrup 2003) fashion has emerged as the new national imagery. In the transformation to knowledge-based societies, the Scandinavian notion of design, of giving form and making things, increasingly seems outdated; it is often referred to in the public discourse as "an old chair." New design policy initiatives stress the importance of new perceptions of design—for example, as a strategic approach to innovation through particular ways of thinking and structuring work processes. At the same time, "outdated" seems to be the watchword of the ideological vision that grew out of the social democratic welfare state, based on equality and democracy for all. Under conditions of globalization, international competitiveness appears to be more important than social ideals, at least in current government rhetoric, as will be later shown.

Even the term "Scandinavia" has lost some of the symbolic significance it carried in the 1950s and 1960s, when it was used in the international promotion of design from Denmark, Norway, Sweden, and Finland. At the time, it linked a particular style of design with the political sphere of the social democratic welfare state, although the Scandinavian countries could not be accurately characterized by political unity either then or now (Østergaard 1997). The preferred term today is the Nordic region, which in geographical terms includes Finland, Iceland, and Greenland as well as Denmark, Norway, and Sweden. However, I use the term Scandinavian here to describe the group of countries that are part of the Scandinavian Peninsula, the geographical area just above Northern Europe. When it comes to fashion, Scandinavia is not considered a collective label suitable for international promotion, as it was in the heyday of Scandinavian design. Denmark, Sweden, and Norway act independently, have their own fashion policies, and think mostly of each other as competitors not only in the region, but also internationally.

The idea of design nation, the starting point of the present analysis, is relatively well-defined. This is not the case for the idea of fashion nation, the model into which the Scandinavian countries may be developing, as my research studies. By stressing "fashion nation," I wish to emphasize how each of the three Scandinavian governments are currently, and for the first time in recent history, taking a sincere interest in fashion design and fashion clothing industries, and formulating policies for them. For each, the fashion industry is seen as critical for success in the new knowledge-based global economy. Fashion is viewed as cosmopolitan and capable of anticipating future trends, as a successful intermediary in globalized production networks, bringing economic gain on the basis of mostly immaterial processes such as branding, marketing, and trade. Unlike the paternalistic appearance of design nations, fashion nations focus not particularly on what is considered good for society and the individual, but on what makes the nation state appear attractive, modern, and forward-looking.

In this article, I unpack what I term the fashion dreams of the Scandinavian countries in order to examine what their experiences tell us—on the one hand, the role of fashion for the nation and, on the other hand, the contribution of national governments to the polycentrism of the fashion world. In the respective cases of Denmark, Sweden, and Norway, I explore the processes by which fashion is inscribed in industry policy, showing in each case how the different outcomes are produced by each country's particular industry conditions and constellations of private and public actor involvement. My overall argument is that the inscription of fashion in national discourse for the construction of a country's image should not only be read as an industry policy measure, whose efficiency can be evaluated in reaching a stated goal. It should equally be seen as an attempt to formulate models for small peripheral countries in Europe in the era of globalization, as a way to bring them into the cosmopolitan consciousness. For a small country the image of fashion is important in getting the attention of fashion consumers, international fashion media, and tourists, but even more so in attracting the investment and participation of knowledge workers and international companies. I use the term "fashion dreams" to designate the complex nature of the Scandinavian governments' engagement in fashion, including uncertain but ambitious hopes and desires for reenergizing national visions.

Before turning to the case studies, I offer a perspective on the complex relationship between fashion and nation that is unique to each case study, and draw attention to the challenges met by governments aiming to mobilize fashion for the nation as a globalization strategy.

## Fashion Nation

Following the globalization of fashion, there has been an increasing interest in the study of fashion in relation to nation, as the dominance of Western fashion has been exchanged for an increasingly "multicultural fashion regime," as Lise Skov has pointed out (2003: 239). However, the research perspectives are numerous and diverse. The interest among some researchers has been in rewriting the history of fashion in order to both recover local histories and replace previous notions of authoritative fashion centers (e.g. Maynard 2001; O'Byrne 2000; Steele 1998; White 2000). Subsequently, these studies contribute to the production of myths and images of distinctiveness. Other studies consciously challenge such myth production (e.g. Breward *et al.* 2002) or try to explain the complexity of the link and its continuous reproduction in practice (e.g. Brand and Teunissen 2005; Craik 2009; Goodrum 2005; Palmer 2004; Skov 2003). In the diverse cases of Hong Kong fashion and British fashion, both Lise Skov (2003) and Alison Goodrum (2005) show how cultural distinctiveness is a complex design intent that functions as a kind of legitimization strategy to gain market position. As further stressed by Brand and Teunissen (2005), local sartorial traditions gain importance as part of these strategic moves for creating difference. Local dress traditions are deconstructed and reinvented to fit contemporary global fashions with touches of cultural specificity.

Where the situation in Scandinavia is concerned, the complexity of the relationship between fashion and nation similarly includes the design issue of creating cultural distinctiveness. However, here there are particular challenges, as the relationship between fashion and nation was inconceivable until recently. After the nineteenth-century National Romantic movement and the nation-state building of independent democracies in Scandinavia,[2] fashion was perceived and practiced as something that came from abroad and formed a part of the cosmopolitan orientation of the elites. Fashion, with its changing styles of dress, was seen to represent the antithesis of the nation-building process, in contrast to particular local peasant festive wear, which was perceived as constant and viewed as a metaphor for the ideas of freedom and equality desired by the young nations (Sørensen and Stråth 1997). As a consequence, festive peasant dress was elevated to national folk dress as part of the nationalist movement (Lorenzen 1987; Stoklund 2003). Romantic genre paintings depicted men and women dressed in folk dresses, popularizing the understanding of national identity in dress as static and resistant to the influence of fashion. Today, using modernist nationalism research, dress historians explain how such clothes were also subject to changing fashions (e.g. Eldvik 2010; Haugen 2006; Lorenzen 1987), but nevertheless they remain popular as a sign of the nation in Sweden and Norway, though less so in Denmark. The use of folk dress at private and public celebrations is particularly common in Norway. This practice also occurs in Sweden, where a specific national costume ("Allmänna Svenska Nationaldräkten") was introduced in 1903 and worn on the National Day, June 6, since its introduction in 1983. In Denmark, the use of folk dress is uncommon, limited to the minor folk dance movement, and as a result the knowledge of this kind of dress, of its manufacture and materials, is limited to folk dancers and dress curators working mainly at cultural historic museums.

In this respect, the Scandinavian countries developed a notion that they had two different kinds of dress. One was folk dress, historically oriented backwards, growing out of preindustrial peasant society and used to signify the nation in a more or less formal and ceremonial way. The other was fashion, seen as future-oriented, connecting citizens with the rest of the world, and viewed as neutral in terms of national significance. However, the relation between the two types of dress is perceived in different ways—in Denmark they are mutually exclusive and folk dress has little place in contemporary life, whereas in Norway they are seen as complementary; national folk dress still has a place in ordinary people's wardrobes and are brought out for festive occasions. Sweden, one could argue, is placed somewhere in between the two extremes.

Therefore, sartorial traditions do not tend to form a strong part of a design strategy in Denmark, but they are more common inspirations in Norway, where traditional knitting patterns are reinterpreted in contemporary fashion design (for example, the brand Arne and Carlos). Jennifer Craik suggests that national fashion "is the expressive encapsulation of the cultural psyche or zeitgeist of a place through its people that occurs when three realms are synchronized: aesthetics, cultural practice and cultural articulation" (Craik 2009: 413); in Denmark, aesthetic distinctiveness or the recognizability of clothing style is the least significant. One could argue the situation is different in Sweden and Norway due to the common use of outdoor wear; although similar dress traditions can be localized in Iceland as well as North America, which makes it hard to argue that outdoor wear is particular Swedish or Norwegian. Further, neither Danish consumers nor Danish fashion designers seem concerned with the representation of the nation through their dress or design practices. In the 1960s and early 1970s, the relationship of fashion and nation mainly addressed the representation of the nation as modern. The design aim was to make something new, appealing to local as well as international consumers and at the same time unique in the sense of the signature design of the individual fashion designer (Melchior 2008). The link between fashion and nation was at times presented by the media as a reflection of the trendy modern Danish, Swedish, or Norwegian lifestyles, but did not result in a clear perception of the cultural distinctiveness of Scandinavian fashion, as was the case for Scandinavian design. Fashion design from Scandinavia could just as easily belong to any country whose fashion designers were informed by the latest Western fashion trends.

Today's new emphasis on the relationship of fashion and nation in the Scandinavian countries seems in keeping with the historical relationship of fashion and nation. Not surprisingly, it is driven neither by particular Scandinavian dress practices nor by self-exoticization of local sartorial tradition, as in the examples by Brand and Teunissen (2005) or Skov (2003). Instead the relationship is government-driven and must be understood in connection to the new conditions of nation-states under globalization. In these conditions, as the ethnologist Søren Christensen has pointed out, national identity and culture are increasingly seen as competitive components for economic development and benefit (Christensen 2006: 81–2). Despite the historical perception that Scandinavian countries are on the receiving end of international fashions, the local fashion industries are now also important producers of national imagery. Fashion is perceived as a suitable means of making the nation stand out internationally by producing fashionable eye-catching clothes and images. It invites and receives attention, which is highly valued by contemporary society on both personal and institutional levels. In the current perspective, fashion can make sense of place, and place branding is a key mission for the nation in a globalized age, in which cities, regions, and countries increasingly compete with one another to attract investors, employees, residents, and tourists (e.g. Anholt 2009; Kavaratzis 2005). The ethnologist Orvar Löfgren has described the longing for the new as a pervasive characteristic of our society. What he terms the "catwalk economy," based on the economic model of launching new ideas twice a year (if not more), is currently being adopted by other industries, from computer to car manufacture, in order to generate more positive awareness and business (Löfgren 2005). My argument is that the Scandinavian governments have joined the catwalk economy. There is a longing for new images today. Through fashion, the Scandinavian countries expect to build their images as outward-looking, internationally influential knowledge societies, which they find necessary in a time of globalization.

Based on existing fashion research literature and on the considerations of the fashion focus in the Scandinavian countries, I think a potential two-way link between fashion and nation should be highlighted. On one hand, fashion companies and the various local fashion industry organizations emphasize cultural distinctiveness and national identity in the design of fashionable clothing, as a commercial strategy to create specificity in the highly competitive international fashion market. On the other hand, governments find it attractive in associating fashion with the image of the nation. Sometimes the two-way link is present at the same time, at other times this is not the case and causes challenges, as the following case studies show.

If the local fashion industry in the nineteenth century was a medium to construct and define the nation state through contemporary folk dresses, among other things; today this industry is considered by local governments to be a suitable partner in a symbolic strategy of redefining and branding the nation as contemporary and part of the new global agenda.

## Great Danes

In the early years of the twenty-first century, the Danish government was the first among the Scandinavian countries to introduce a fashion policy, characterized by ambition and self-confidence. Since 2005, government fashion policy has stated the future potential of the Danish fashion industry to make Denmark/Copenhagen the fifth global fashion center in the world, after Paris, Milan, New York, and London. In its first five years the policy has attracted the local attention of the industry and further government initiatives, rather than realizing the ultimate dream through an international breakthrough.

### The Danish Fashion Industry

In order to understand the Danish case, I shall introduce the Danish fashion industry. The industry is estimated to consist of about 1,200 companies, of which approximately 620 companies are registered by Statistics Denmark as "whole sellers of clothing" (Deloitte 2008; FORA 2005). The majority of these are small companies, owner-managed, with four to nine full-time employees. In total, the industry employed approximately 11,328 people in Denmark as of 2008. In the same year, the industry had an annual turnover of 23.6 billion DKK (3.17 billion euros), of which about 90 percent was gained on export (21.4 billion DKK/2.87 billion euros). However, as in many Western European countries, most of the fashion export can be accounted for by the re-export of clothing produced abroad, and therefore has a low impact on local employment numbers. The main export markets for the Danish fashion industry are the immediate neighboring countries: Germany, Sweden, and Norway (DTB 2008: 2–3).

Yet, the numerous small companies do not drive the economy of the Danish fashion industry. The three largest companies, Bestseller A/S,[3] BTX Group A/S,[4] and IC Companys A/S,[5] are jointly estimated to generate 75 percent of the annual export turnover. These companies are built as concept houses or multi-brand companies and have their own retail distribution network. In particular, Bestseller and BTX can be characterized as primarily price-focused, consisting of market-driven brands with an impersonal design profile. By contrast, IC Companys has a brand portfolio divided into designer-profiled fashion brands—among them the fashion brands By Malene Birger,[6] Designers Remix,[7] and InWear[8]—and fashion brands without a specific designer profile, such as Jackpot, Part Two, Matinique, and Cottonfield.

By combining the export figures of the clothing industry with the Danish textile and leather goods industries, local media and industry trade organizations often call the Danish fashion industry the fourth largest Danish export industry among the country's manufacturing industries.[9] For the last ten years, this has been the continuing success story of the industry. However, business reports show that during the same period fewer than half of the industry's companies has generated profits (Deloitte 2008, 2009).

Despite this mixture of success and failure, the political awareness of the Danish fashion industry has developed over the last decade. Before this, the government did not pay any specific attention to the fashion industry. It was considered a sunset industry that would quietly disappear when left to its own devices, especially in the late 1980s with lay-offs of local seamstresses, pattern cutters, knitters, and other skilled workers, forcing companies to close or outsource their production. But instead of disappearing, the Danish fashion industry was, in a European context, an early adaptor to globalization. Since the 1970s, production has gradually been outsourced to low-cost countries in Europe and Asia, and the industry has locally been transformed and given a new focus on design, branding, marketing, and retail.

Today most Danish fashion companies show their collections biannually at the fashion week in Copenhagen. Copenhagen Fashion Week has existed since the late 1950s and, in the last ten to fifteen years, has developed into a major fashion week in the Scandinavian region with predominantly Danish and Northern European visitors. At fashion week it is possible to see some of the best known Danish designer fashion brands, including Bruuns Bazaar, By Malene Birger, Day Birger et Mikkelsen, Munthe + Simonsen, Baum und Pferdgarten, Samsøe & Samsøe, Designers Remix, InWear, Mads Nørgaard Copenhagen, Rützou, Noir, Henrik Vibskov, and Stine Goya. It is difficult to discern a common identity among these brands, an observation also made in the 2004 exhibition *Unik Danish Fashion* at the Danish Center for Design (Malling and Most 2004). Danish fashion brands vary from a cosmopolitan classic look (e.g. Bruuns Bazaar; Figure 1) and bohemian and ethnic-inspired styles (e.g. Munthe plus Simonsen and Day Birger et Mikkelsen) to avant-garde street styles (e.g. Henrik Vibskov and Stine Goya). Despite the different looks, there is a consensus on Danish fashion as wearable, affordable, and in tune with international trends, in that respect representing what is proudly termed democratic fashion or simply described as "good value for money" (Rasmussen 2006).

## Denmark/Copenhagen—The Fifth Global Fashion Center

Why did the fashion industry catch the attention of the Danish government, then liberal-conservative, at the beginning of the twenty-first

**Figure 1**
The Danish fashion brand Bruuns Bazaar presenting its Spring/Summer 2007 collection at Copenhagen Fashion Week. Bruuns Bazaar is known for its modern classic style for the urban man and woman. The brand was among the first in the early 1990s to mark the transition of the Danish fashion industry from production based to design based. Image courtesy of Marie Riegels Melchior (photographer).

century, giving life to the dream of Denmark/Copenhagen becoming the fifth global fashion center?

I think the answers to this question lie in the developments of the industry as previously described: it is considered a successful industry, which has continued to grow after deindustrialization. However, it is possible to see more specifically why the government formulated its fashion policy by reading its self-initiated report from 2005, entitled "User-driven innovation in Danish fashion—the fifth global fashion center?" ("Brugerdreven innovation i dansk mode—den 5. globale modeklynge?"; see also FORA 2003).

The report argued for the importance of user-driven innovation in the fashion industry, demonstrating the fashion industry's involvement in the overall Danish industry policy. In 2005, user-driven innovation was introduced as a key asset at which the Danes excel, and for some years Denmark's stated goal was to become "the most innovative country in the world"—particularly with regard to user-driven innovation (Innovationsrådet 2005: 5). User-driven innovation was, in other words, seen as a key Danish characteristic and as a potential for future development referencing research findings that foreigners associated user-friendliness, good design, and simplicity with Denmark and the Danes. This concept was introduced not only as an innovation method but also as a cultural characteristic and a political buzzword, believed to strengthen the competitiveness of local industries on global markets. But it was not clear what user-driven innovation could actually do for the Danish fashion industry, besides calling for more focus on its specificity to differentiate it from its competitors and project a stronger and more independent image of Denmark.

Based on structural studies of the leading international fashion centers of Paris, New York, London, and Milan, as classified in the report, it was declared that the implementation of the Danish fashion policy required the industry to secure its critical mass, achieve stronger coherence among industry companies, and operate as a center. The industry needed to strengthen the education of fashion designers, develop the business knowledge of the industry, provide a "knowledge center" for the industry (like Future Concept Labs in Milan or the Cultural Access Group in New York), and build a network organization. Finally, the report stated the importance of differentiating Denmark's fashion industry from those of other countries by emphasizing its strengths and characteristics (FORA 2005: 60–2).

In subsequent years, the recommendations of the government's fashion policy were followed by the establishment of the network organization *Danish Fashion Institute* in late 2005 by joint government and industry support. From the beginning, the aim of the organization has been to coordinate and promote the exciting biannual fashion week in Copenhagen under the new brand name *Copenhagen Fashion Week* (Figure 2), as well as to promote and strengthen the perception of a

**Figure 2**
Copenhagen Fashion Week, February 2007. During the event the City Hall of Copenhagen was transformed into the center stage for fashion shows presenting the Fall/Winter 2007/8 collections. Once the initiative of the Danish Fashion Institute, the previously exclusive industry fashion shows have, since 2006, become public events as wide screens are placed at different locations in the city center to attract ordinary people's interest in fashion. Image courtesy of Marie Riegels Melchior (photographer).

specific Danish fashion through industry seminars, assistance for start-ups, support of exhibitions, fashion awards, fashion design talent scouting, etc. Some of this work was already handled by the major trade organization, *Dansk Fashion & Textile*, and the emergence of a new organization has led to some tension between the organizations. While the government favors Danish Fashion Institute for promotional work for the industry, the trade organization feels it has the mandate of the industry, though without a history of direct government collaboration.

Since 2005, the government fashion policy has been further developed and supported by initiatives. For example, in 2008 the director of Danish Fashion Institute was appointed as board member of the newly established *Foundation for the Promotion of Denmark* (in Danish, "Fonden til Markedsføringen af Danmark"); later that same year, Danish Fashion Institute was again appointed by the ministry to coordinate the initiative of "The Fashion Zone," with the aim of strengthening the Danish fashion industry through stronger cohesion. So far, the outcome of the initiative has been the establishment of a website publishing news and information about the Danish fashion industry and organizing knowledge-sharing events.[10]

## Challenges for the Government's Fashion Policy

Until now, the government's fashion policy has led to a stronger public awareness of the industry, mainly driven by the network organization and its strong skills in communications. But the effort has primarily been local and international recognition is still waiting to be pursued. Attempts to identify the Danishness of Danish fashion have also been made, but no clear answer has been found besides the democratic quality of Danish fashion given its price point and wearability (Rasmussen 2006). As I see it, this is due to the historical lack of a national perception of dress in Denmark. Consumers are not demanding national specificity, and Danish fashion designers are neither trained in what are the local sartorial traditions nor trying to represent the nation through the making of clothes. Their enterprise is transnational and in reality fashion designers and other stakeholders have not been very interested.

The fashion policy faces further challenges in attempting to unite the whole industry around it in order to work to reach its goal. Recurring disagreements between the trade organization (representing the industry) and the Danish Fashion Institute (mainly representing the government) have been reported in the Danish media. For example, the trade organization announced that the policy was misdirecting the focus of the industry, when it was actually necessary to earn money on the core business of making clothes through trading. As they stated, it must be accepted that Denmark is a "trade nation," not a "couture nation."[11]

## Great Dreams

As a fashion industry policy, the idea of the fifth global fashion center has been highly ambivalent. On one hand, it is based on a glaring misreading of Denmark's potential in global fashion. As David Gilbert pointed out in his introduction to *Fashion's World Cities* (2006), Tokyo is already considered the fifth global fashion center, and Shanghai aspires to be the sixth global fashion center. There is a whole row of large competitive fashion nations. Therefore, in terms of international recognition, it has been embarrassing for a small country to push this slogan. On the other hand, it must be acknowledged that the policy has been productive on the domestic scene in creating visibility for the fashion industry and mobilizing networks of consultants, media people, researchers, and educators. Of course, it has also caused confusion in the industry; ultimately, the policy is connected to great dreams rather than reality.

Perhaps the policy makers and involved organizations were wise to avoid defining specific success criteria for the first Danish fashion policy. This has spared them the unpleasant moment of awakening to reality. Instead, it seems possible that Denmark or Copenhagen can be a self-proclaimed fashion center if it wants to be. This shows the distance between the policy rhetoric and the industry whose interests it supposedly advances. In reality, many Danish fashion companies are struggling to simply stay in business, especially after the 2008 financial crisis. While they do not believe that the fashion policy was formulated to serve their interests, as I see it, they have been willing to give voice to the importance of Danish fashion as long as it is a political priority.

## Strong Swedes

The biggest difference between the Danish and Swedish fashion industries is the fact that Sweden is home to one of the world's major and most successful fashion companies, Hennes & Mauritz AB (H&M). H&M operates in thirty-four countries, employs about 73,000 people, and in 2008 had a turnover of 104 billion SEK (72.2 billion DKK/9.62 billion euros).[12] H&M alone is three times bigger than the entire Danish industry. With this in mind, it is hardly surprising that fashion features prominently in the official "face" of Sweden. In the portrait gallery welcoming fliers to Arlanda Airport near Stockholm, among famous Swedes such as Alfred Nobel, Ingmar Bergman, Ingrid Bergman, tennis player Björn Borg and the royal family, one can also find fashion designers, CEOs, and founders of major Swedish fashion companies (Figure 3).[13] Fashion also has come into focus for Swedish museums, such as Stockholm's Nordiska Museet, which in 2010 opened the permanent exhibition *The Power of Fashion: 300 years of Clothing*, and at Stockholm University even an independent program since 2006 has developed under the heading "Centre for Fashion Studies." Although the Swedish fashion policy also contains

**Figure 3**
As one arrives at Arlanda Airport outside the Swedish capital of Stockholm from abroad, the "Stockholm hall of fame" portrait wall welcomes you. From pictures of the present royal family members, successful sportsmen, and business people, to significant historic individuals, the people who built Sweden are evident. This includes fashion designers, such as, to the right, Jonny Johansson, founder and creative director of the international acclaimed jeans brand Acne A/B. Image courtesy of Marie Riegels Melchior (photographer).

aspirational elements, it is grounded in both industry interests and cultural interests, and has more realistic goals than its Danish counterpart. Sweden's current fashion dream is to take part in the design of a new progressive Sweden.

### The Swedish Fashion Industry

According to economist Atle Hauge, the industry is dominated by retail chains, with H&M as the largest (Hauge 2007: 29); but it also has a few smaller wholesale fashion companies with current international recognition, including the fashion brands of Acne, Filippa K, J. Lindeberg, Whyred, Hope, and Nudie Jeans. In total, the Swedish fashion industry consisted in 2003 of about 1,500 companies. Like the Danish case, the Swedish fashion industry is an export industry, with the other Nordic countries ranking as its main markets; the industry export is estimated at about 6 billion SEK (650 million euros) and the local turnover at 64.4 billion SEK (6.98 billion euros), of which H&M is responsible for 5.3 billion SEK (570 million euros) and Lindex AB (though less branded than H&M), for 3.3 billion SEK (360 million euros).[14] In the latter half of the twentieth century, local manufacturing was outsourced to low-wage countries in Europe and Asia; what remains in Sweden is, as in Denmark, a knowledge-based industry of design, branding, marketing, and retail. With this transition, the Swedish government has taken interest in the industry, but not as strongly as in Denmark. Specifically, the awareness of the fashion industry is due to the success of H&M, but also acknowledges the economic potential of fashion in general. Fashion designs are believed to hold unique potential for the branding of Sweden abroad, as stated in the government initiative report "Fashion Sweden: A Survey of Swedish Fashion Design" ("Mode Svea: En genomlysning av svensk modedesign") (Sundberg 2006: 9).

Swedish fashion is generally characterized by functional clothes based on sober design, as stated by trend forecaster Cay Bond (2006). This perception of Swedish fashion has its roots in the 1960s development of the Swedish fashion industry, but in recent years it has been questioned by the exposure of new Swedish fashion companies representing a wide variety of style. In 2005, Dunkers Kulturhus in Helsingborg (in southern Sweden), the fashion exhibition *In Fashion: New Swedish Clothing Design* emphasized, among other things, "how [...] multifaced Swedish fashion currently is [...]" (Carelli and Wilhelmsson 2005: 5). For fashion designers and fashion people it is somehow challenging to look for a common identity of Swedish fashion. Even so, in contrast to the situation in Denmark, fashion companies are far more likely to label their clothes as "Designed in Sweden." The fashion industry appears to be responding to globalization's demand for marks of local originality. Labeling Swedish fashionable clothing as "Designed in Sweden" does not conflict with any particular style. It is believed to be a technical statement, not a symbolic statement linked to cultural distinctiveness.

### Fashion as Image of a New Progressive Sweden

Although the Swedish industry has not yet experienced the same level of government involvement as its Danish counterpart, in the last five years there has been a growing government interest in the industry, including the publication of the earlier mentioned report. The report makes several points, the most salient being that the domination of the industry by retail chains has made it difficult for new fashion brands to enter the market. As a consequence, new fashion companies often have a short life span. Another point in the report is the lack of a collective strategy for the industry. There are many different institutions and organizations concerned with the Swedish fashion industry, from educational institutions, industry and trade organizations, to export councils and trend forecasting agencies. Yet, according to the report, the problem is that they operate individually, and as a consequence the industry does not have the coordinated strategy that is necessary for securing further growth and realizing the potential to represent the nation as desired. The report examined one possible solution to this problem by asking a selection of Swedish fashion companies if they wanted more collective promotion of "Swedish fashion" based on government support. The majority of the fashion companies' answers were skeptical. Small companies saw such an initiative as shortsighted; for them, it is not enough to receive financial support to exhibit at a foreign fashion fair. As expected, they expressed a need for long-term investment and support regarding strategic planning to help them enter new markets and establish serious contacts with foreign buyers as well as press. Other companies, of different sizes, found mutual promotion initiatives under the heading "Swedish fashion" to be problematic, as for them Swedishness is not a common denominator; it is more important for them to communicate their individual identities in order to consolidate brand and business platforms (Sundberg 2006: 50). The companies' reaction highlights the common problem of co-branding—in this case, fashion companies promoted as "Swedish fashion" are dependent on the positive brand value of Sweden, which they are not empowered to control (Aaker 1995).

A few years later, *The Swedish Institute*, a government-funded agency working to promote Swedish interests abroad, and *Visit Sweden*, a public organization targeting tourism in Sweden, took further interest in the Swedish fashion industry. The Swedish Institute declared one of its focus areas to be "new creativity," in the sense of pioneering contemporary culture and creative industries, seen as the manifestation of "the new progressive Sweden."[15] The exhibition *Swedish Fashion—Exploring a New Identity*, shown at the Fashion and Textile Museum in London in Spring 2009, was part of this initiative. Its aim was to expose the new progressive Sweden by showing fashion designers that have particularly challenged the stereotypical notion of Swedish fashion as functional clothes. In other words, contemporary fashion design was an attempt to show a new Swedish image and communicate distance from the traditional Swedish aesthetic corresponding to the values of the twentieth-century Swedish welfare state.

*Visit Sweden*'s further engagement with the Swedish fashion industry was officially initiated in late 2009 with the launch of *Association of Swedish Fashion Brands*, which since has received a donation of 1 million SEK (110,000 euros) from the government to promote Swedish fashion. The association was founded through a collaboration of Swedish fashion brands—Filippa K, Tiger of Sweden, Cheap Monday, Whyred, and Hope—with the newspaper *Bon*, the PR agency Patriksson Communication, and *Visit Sweden*. The aim of the association is to strengthen the Swedish fashion industry and increase its visibility in order to promote Sweden and its capital Stockholm, primarily through the coordination of the Mercedes Benz Fashion Week held in the capital biannually.[16]

Compared to the Danish case, it is clear that Swedish government involvement is less aggressive. The government has explored what characterizes fashion in Sweden, leading to their current investment in the fashion industry through industry collaborations regarding the branding of Sweden. The fashion industry is perceived as an image-maker of Sweden, transforming the image of the nation towards the new rather than projecting a specific national style through the sum of the country's fashion design. The Swedish government is not aiming to turn the country or its capital into a global fashion center, as is the ambition of the Danish government, but more modestly to develop through fashion a new image of the nation, which makes its fashion dream strong in realistic terms.

This focus on image-making ties nicely into the cultural developments concerning fashion at museums and at Stockholm University and make it more realistic to believe in the Swedish fashion dream coming true. Even though the university program of Fashion Studies is made possible by a significant donation from the founder of H&M, Erling Persson Family Foundation, it facilitates research and educational programs that are less oriented towards industry knowledge, but more on fashion as a cultural and artistic form of expression, the same way that fashion is recognized by the government agenda. It is most likely that the initiative will affect both the general level of understanding of fashion as a cultural phenomenon and, with candidates obtaining jobs in the fashion industry's marketing departments, the potential to strengthen company profiles for further international recognition.

## Brave Norwegians

The case of Norway it is very different from both Denmark and Sweden. The Norwegian fashion industry is small, and international recognition of Norwegian fashion brands is even more limited than that of its Scandinavian counterparts. Some people might know of the Norwegian fashion designer Per Spook (b. 1939), who had an international fashion designer career in Paris in the 1960s and 1970s as chief designer of the fashion house Louis Féraud, and ran his own *haute couture* fashion house from 1977 to 1995, or recognize the country's knitwear tradition and sports- and outdoor wear, with international brands such as Helly Hansen (established 1877) or Swix Sport (established 1943).

Nevertheless, Norway has most recently formulated its fashion policy with clear influence from the government fashion focus in both Denmark and Sweden (Nordgård *et al.* 2008: 16). In 2008 Norsk Form (The Foundation for Design and Architecture in Norway), a government-initiated institution, published the report "Fashion Pilot: An Investigation of the Norwegian Field of Fashion Design" ("Motepilot: En undersøkelse av det norske motedesignfeltet"), which did not merely describe the industry but also explored it and its future potential for the first time (Nordgård *et al.* 2008: 13).

## The Norwegian Fashion Industry

The 2008 report characterized the Norwegian fashion industry as a minor industry, with little coherence, which has yet to be discovered and understood (Nordgård *et al.* 2008: 13, 70–1). Based on 2005 statistics, the Norwegian fashion industry is comprised of 1,140 whole sellers of textile, clothing, and footwear (Nordgård *et al.* 2008: 34).[17] These companies collectively employ about 4,213 people, and had an annual turnover of 14.5 billion NOK (1.79 billion euros) in 2005. Many are one-man or one-woman companies, and most are directed at the domestic market. New Norwegian fashion brands that caught attention locally are, among others, Fam Irvoll, Arne & Carlos, Batlak og Selvig, and Cecilie Melli.

The annual export of Norwegian fashion is therefore very limited in comparison to its Scandinavian neighbors. In 2006 it reached 590 million NOK (72.9 million euros). In the same year, the import of fashionable clothing was more than twenty times the size of the export, reaching 12.8 billion NOK (1.5 billion euros). The commercial capability of the Norwegian fashion industry seems to be in fashion retail, dominated by the company Varner Gruppen AS (established in 1962).[18] In summary, the Norwegian fashion industry is regarded as a small industry but believed to have growth potential, specifically in the export market (Nordgård *et al.* 2008: 70).

## Norwegian Fashion Design—A Well-Known Brand

The 2008 report claims the existence of a Norwegian fashion focus, despite the small size of the industry. At the same time, the report calls for stronger recognition of the industry by the government for its growth potential. Additionally, the report concludes that further coherence and a more robust network must be implemented by government initiative in order to establish a self-conscious Norwegian fashion industry (Nordgård *et al.* 2008: 68–9). The report advised the establishment of a *Norwegian Fashion Institute*, following the Danish example. This suggestion was realized in February 2009 with financial support from the government and initiated by "Innovasjon Norge."

Through the Norwegian Fashion Institute, a Norwegian fashion policy was formulated. One of its first initiatives was the promotion of Norwegian fashion during Expo 2010 in Shanghai, as part of the contemporary image of Norway. The initiative, aligned with the stated fashion policy of making Norwegian fashion a well-known fashion brand, will specifically focus on the promotion of a Norwegian fashion identity. This approach differs significantly from those taken by both Denmark and Sweden and takes advantage of Norway's unique dress history. National folk dress is still in use by many Norwegians, and this perhaps constitutes a stronger common ground for Norwegian fashion designers to address the Norwegian fashion identity. Still, the government-initiated report did not go into detail in describing the content of a Norwegian fashion identity, other than references to knitting and the country's popular tradition of wearing clothing perceived as national folk dress ("bunad"; Figure 4). The national sartorial traditions dating

**Figure 4**
Dressing for the nation at Norway's National Day, May 17. For the parade in front of the Royal Castle in Oslo, Norwegians gather to celebrate the nation, some dressed up in so-called "bunad," some new and some old, inherited from family members. Image courtesy of Bjørn Sverre Hol Haugen (photographer).

back to the nineteenth century are, in other words, still considered to be foundational for a contemporary Norwegian fashion brand.

The Norwegian Fashion Institute has also gone in another direction by taking the lead of the Nordic project *NICE* (Nordic Initiative Clean and Ethical),[19] which aims at promoting ethical and sustainable business practices in the region. This indicates a strong value-driven vision, and unlike the Danish and Swedish initiatives there is no attempt at claiming leadership of the region. One of the highly successful projects under the NICE initiative concerns the use of Norwegian wool for fashion production. With wool as a key material of Norwegian knitwear and folk dress, the project shows how in various ways cultural distinctiveness and ethics is tied into the Norwegian fashion discourse in contrast to both the other cases.

But still the Norwegian fashion policy faces the challenge of getting recognition, particularly internationally without any front-running companies. As in the Danish case, the initiated fashion policy may have better odds locally than internationally. The Norwegian fashion dream is more modest than those of Denmark or Sweden: Norway does not proclaim itself to be a leading regional center, but simply aims to improve the recognition of Norwegian fashion domestically and overseas. In terms of the cultural claim to being a fashion nation, Norway is also more reluctant to claim a role as producer of cosmopolitan fashion. Instead, it draws on some of its complementary traditions of national folk dresses and outdoor activities. These in turn can be used as sources of cultural distinctiveness, as in other countries responding to increased competition caused by the globalization of fashion production and consumption. As such Norwegian fashion is likewise believed to boost the imagery of the nation, but due to the premises it is a brave ambition.

## Conclusion: Scandinavian Fashion Nations?

With the terms "great Danes," "strong Swedes," and "brave Norwegians," I try to paraphrase the specificity of the fashion policies of the Scandinavian countries. As I have already stated, "great Danes" refers to the recognition of the Danish fashion industry as a significant export industry, and the highly self-confident ambition of the Danish government to make Denmark/Copenhagen the fifth global fashion center. But it also refers to the great distance from dream to reality, as it entails a failure to understand the challenges of becoming a leading global fashion center, stemming from Danish provinciality. In reality, this improbable dream has so far only been productive for the local mobilization of the Danish fashion industry, attracting local attention and perhaps boosting the self-confidence and self-consciousness of the industry with the possible outcome of greater sales and export. "Strong Swedes" refers to the already strong market position of the Swedish fashion industry in international fashion, as well as the achievability of the Swedish government's ambition to support the fashion industry in order to associate itself with the new image of a progressive, modern, cosmopolitan, and up-to-date Sweden. Finally, "brave Norwegians" refers to a minor fashion industry that, despite its size, lack of coherence, and, until recently, government recognition, is sufficiently daring and courageous to want to enter international markets and become a well-known fashion brand.

In all three cases, it is clear that the fashion dreams are highly government-driven. The Scandinavian countries share a common belief in fashion as a strategy to support the image of the nation, particularly an imagery that differs from the previous idea of Scandinavian design nations. In both Denmark and Sweden, the images delivered by the fashion industry and the designs of its companies are not nationally focused. It is in tune with international fashion and, at best, represents an independent brand identity that falls in between classic European dressing styles and avant-garde-invoked street style. The case of Norway is a little different, as the image of the nation through fashion still makes reference to national identity through self-exoticizing design strategies.

But with the emphasis on fashion, the focus is more about what is trendy and attention-grabbing, and less about stronger ideological visions. The Scandinavian countries demand international attention through fashion—it is the attention they are after, not the communication of a particular message, as far as I see it. At least, as the case studies have demonstrated, neither the fashion industries nor the fashion design they deliver have something particular to say apart from being fashionable.

At the beginning of this article, I asked whether the Scandinavian countries are transforming their cultural significance from design nations to fashion nations. I think I dare answer the question with a yes. The countries have not dismissed the role of design endeavors apart from fashion, but their contribution is not intended to communicate or materialize certain political visions of defining the good life for all. Governments form partnerships with the fashion industry, according to the case studies discussed, in the hopes of being perceived as trendy, modern, and hip nation states. However, this strategy could also be a dangerous trajectory to follow. It seems a peculiar decision for a government to associate itself with an industry that adjusts oversupply by supplying novelty to an uncontrollably consumerist audience, and further that outsources irresponsible use of national resources and extremely poor labor conditions (child labor, unpaid overwork, poor safety, etc.). Further if the dream is too unrealistic, detached from practice, and therefore unachievable, as at least in the Danish case, it easily undermines the original idea. Among the industry players, it perhaps creates more confusion than confidence. But despite that it also has the potential to enable a local fashion industry to become more reflective on the relationship of fashion and nation in which they play a part, and to find answers for new ways of structuring the industry and new ways that fashion nation can become a creative potential for the design of clothing. The three case studies are just not there yet.

But the case studies have shown how fashion is believed to be a model for small nations to enter the global arena. It feeds into the idea of a polycentric fashion world and throws light on how it is reproduced not only through commerce and consumption, but also through government policies and nation-states searching for new ways for being and being seen on the global stage of the current globalized world.

## Notes

1. This article is founded in my PhD dissertation on Danish fashion (Melchior 2008). The article is characteristic of a Scandinavian comparative perspective basis made possible by the study of government initiative reports, websites, and secondary literature on contemporary Danish, Swedish, and Norwegian fashion industries. Due to my more in-depth knowledge of the Danish case, I have decided to let the case study begin the article and form the basis of the comparison with the Swedish and Norwegian cases.
2. In 1849 the absolutist monarchy was abolished in Denmark, in 1866 in Sweden, and in 1905 Norway declared its independence after centuries belonging to the Danish Kingdom and, since 1814, to the Kingdom of Sweden.
3. Bestseller A/S (est. 1979) had in 2007 an annual turnover of 10.4 billion DKK (1.38 billion euros) and employed 2,654 people in Denmark. The company represents ten different fashion brands for children, women, and menswear, including the brands Vero Moda and Jack & Jones. In 2007 the company ran 1,740 own-concept stores (www.bestseller.com).
4. BTX Group A/S (est. 2005 when the capital fund EQT bought the company Brandtex A/S, est. 1935) had in 2008 an annual turnover of 3.194 billion DKK (430 million euros) and employs 1,593 people. The company represents nineteen different fashion brands for teenagers, women, and menswear, including the brands b.young and Blend (www.btx-group.dk).
5. IC Companys A/S (est. 2001 by the merger of InWear A/S (est. 1969) and Carli Gry International A/S (est. 1973)) represents eleven different fashion brands for women and menswear. In 2006 the company's annual turnover was 3.023 billion DKK (410 million euros), it employed 2,200 people, and ran 259 concept stores. The company is publicly listed on the Copenhagen Stock Exchange (www.iccompanies.dk).
6. The head of design of By Malene Birger is Malene Birger, who founded the company in 2003. Until 2010 the company was partly owned by Malene Birger, but is now owned solely by IC Companys.

7. Designer and Creative Director of Designers Remix is Charlotte Eskildsen.
8. InWear's current Design Manager is Lene Borggaard. The brand was established in 1969 as a fashion design brand with Kirsten Teisner as head designer. During the early 1980s, Teisner left the brand and for more than two decades its designer profile was anonymous until Borggaard was introduced as the brand's designer profile in 2007.
9. Based on 2003 figures, the export profit of the fashion industry (i.e. the export of clothing, textile, and leather goods) was 30 billion DKK (4.02 billion euros), making it the fourth largest manufacturing export industry, next to the medical industry as the third largest (export profit of 32.1 billion DKK/4.31 billion euros), the agricultural industry as the second largest (export profit of 67.9 billion DKK/9.11 billion euros), and the electronic and machine industry as the largest (export profit of 92.1 billion DKK/12.35 billion euros; FORA 2005: 14).
10. See www.fashionforum.dk.
11. See the newspaper article in *Børsen* (February 10, 2010: 6).
12. H&M Annual Report 2008.
13. Among the portraits are of Jonny Johansson (founder of Acne AB), Mikael Shiller (CEO of Acne AB), Erling Persson (founder of Hennes & Mauritz AB), and Filippa Knutsson (founder of Filippa K AB). Observation made November 5, 2009.
14. These numbers are based on 2005 statistics (Sundberg 2006: 13).
15. www.si.se/English/Navigation/About-SI/Focus-areas-2007-2010/ (accessed December 16, 2009).
16. www.modeakrivet.se (accessed December 16, 2009).
17. It has not been possible to find the exclusive number of fashion companies focusing solely on clothing to compare with the Danish and Swedish cases.
18. Varner Gruppen AS has since 1967 been known for its retail concept under the brand name of Dressmann. Since 1980 the company developed as a conglomerate, owning and running a bicycle factory, an insurance agency, real estate, as well as manufacturing of workwear (www.varner.no).
19. www.nicefashion.org (accessed November 30, 2010).

## References

Aaker, David A. 1995. *Building Strong Brands*. New York: The Free Press.

Anholt, Simon. 2009. *Places. Identity, Image and Reputation*. Basingstoke: Palgrave Macmillan.

Bond, Cay. 2006. *New Fashion in Sweden*. Stockholm: Svenska Institutet.

Brand, Jan and Josè Teunissen (eds). 2005. *Global Fashion / Local Tradition: On the Globalisation of Fashion*. Arnhem: Terra.

Breward, Christopher, Becky Conekin and Caroline Cox (eds). 2002. *The Englishness of English Dress*. Oxford: Berg.

Carelli, Peter and Lena Wilhelmsson (eds). 2005. *På Modet. Ny svensk klädsdesign*. Helsingborg: Dunkers Kulturhus.

Christensen, Søren. 2006. "Danskhed i verdensklasse." In *KRITIK*, #182, pp. 80–94. Copenhagen: Gyldendal.

Craik, Jennifer. 2009. "Is Australian Fashion and Dress Distinctively Australian?" *Fashion Theory* 13(4): 409–41.

Davies, Kevin M. 2003. "Marketing Ploy or Democratic Ideal? On the Mythology of Scandinavian Design." In: Widar Halén and Kerstin Wickman (eds) *Scandinavian Design Beyond the Myth: Fifty Years of Design from the Nordic Countries*, pp. 101–110. Stockholm: Arvinius Förlag/Form Förlag.

Deloitte. 2008. *Analyse af beklædningsbranchen—tendenser og udfordringer*. Copenhagen: Deloitte.

Deloitte. 2009. *Analyse af beklædningsbranchen—tendenser og udfordringer*. Copenhagen: Deloitte.

Dickson, Thomas. 2006. *Dansk Design*. Copenhagen: Gyldendal.

DTB. 2008. *Årsberetning 2007*. Herning: Dansk Textil & Beklædning.

Eldvik, Berit. 2010. *The Power of Fashion: 300 Years of Clothing*. Stockholm: Nordiska Museet.

FORA. 2003. *Sammenligning af danske og udenlandske rammebetingelser og innovationssystemer inden for modebranchen*. Copenhagen: Økonomi- og Erhvervsministeriets enhed for erhvervsforskning og analyse (FORA).

FORA. 2005. *Brugerdreven innovation i dansk mode—den femte globale modeklynge?* Copenhagen: Økonomi- og Erhvervsministeriets enhed for erhvervsforskning og analyse (FORA).

Gilbert, David. 2006. "From Paris to Shanghai: The Changing Geographies of Fashion's World Cities." In Christopher Breward and David Gilbert (eds) *Fashion's World Cities*, pp. 1–32. Oxford: Berg.

Goodrum, Alison. 2005. *The National Fabric: Fashion, Britishness, Globalization*. Oxford: Berg.

Halén, Widar and Kerstin Wickman (eds). 2003. *Scandinavian Design beyond the Myth*. Stockholm: Arvinius Förlag/Form Förlag.

Hauge, Atle. 2007. "Dedicated Followers of Fashion: An Economic Geographic Analysis of the Swedish Fashion Industry." PhD dissertation, *Geografiska Regionsstudier*, no. 76, Uppsala University.

Haugen, Bjørn Sverre Hol (ed.). 2006. *Norsk bunadleksikon*. Oslo: Damm.

Højrup, Thomas. 2003. *Livsformer og velfærdsstat ved en korsvej?* Copenhagen: Museum Tusculanums Press.

Innovationsrådet. 2005. *Innovationscharter for Danmark*. Copenhagen: Innovationsrådet.

Kavaratzis, Michael. 2005. "Place Branding: A Review of Trends and Conceptual Models." *The Marketing Review* 5(4): 329–42.

Lorenzen, Erna. 1987. *Hvem sagde nationaldragt?* Århus: Worianum.

Löfgren, Orvar. 2005. "Catwalking af Coolhunting: The Production of Newness." In: Orvar Löfgren and Robert Willim (eds) *Magic, Culture and the New Economy*, pp. 57–72. Oxford: Berg.

Malling, Malene and Henrik Most (eds). 2004. *Unik: Danish Fashion*. Copenhagen: Malling Publications.

Maynard, Margaret. 2001. *Out of Line: Australian Women and Style*. Sydney: University of New South Wales Press.

Melchior, Marie Riegels. 2008. "Dansk på mode! En undersøgelse af design, identitet og historie i dansk modeindustri." PhD dissertation, The Danish School of Design and the Danish Museum of Art & Design, Copenhagen.

Nordgård, Karun, Karin Fensgård and Sivv Marina Flø Karlsen. 2008. *Motepilot: En undersøkelse av det norske motedesignfeltet*. Oslo: Norsk Form.

O'Byrne, Robert. 2000. *After a Fashion: A History of the Irish Fashion Industry*. Dublin: Town House.

Rasmussen, Thomas Schødt. 2006. *Dansk Mode. Design, Identitet, Historie*. Copenhagen: MOKO.

Palmer, Alexandra (ed). 2004. *Fashion: A Canadian Perspective*. Toronto: University of Toronto Press.

Skov, Lise. 2003. "Fashion-Nation: A Japanese Globalization Experience and a Hong Kong Dilemma." In Carla Jones, Ann-Marie Leshkowich and Sandra Niessen (eds) *Re-Orienting Fashion: The Globalization of Asian Fashion*, pp. 215–43. Oxford: Berg.

Steele, Valerie. 1998. *Paris Fashion*. Oxford: Berg.

Stoklund, Bjarne. 2003. *Tingenes kulturhistorie*. Copenhagen: Museum Tusculanums Forlag.

Sundberg, Göran. 2006. *Mode Svea: En genomlysning av svensk modedesign*. Stockholm: Rådet för arkitektur, form och design/Utbildnings- och Kulturdepartementet.

Sørensen, Øystein and Bo Stråth (eds). 1997. *The Culture Construction of Norden*. Oslo: Scandinavian University Press.

White, Nicola. 2000. *Reconstructing Italian Fashion*. Oxford: Berg.

Østergaard, Uffe. 1997. "The Geopolitics of Nordic Identity." In Øystein Sørensen and Bo Stråth (eds) *The Cultural Construction of Norden*, pp. 25–71. Oslo: Scandinavian University Press.

*Fashion Theory,* Volume 15, Issue 2, pp. 201–224
DOI: 10.2752/175174111X12954359478726
Reprints available directly from the Publishers.
Photocopying permitted by licence only.

# Creativity in the Margins: Identity and Locality in Ireland's Fashion Journey

**Síle de Cléir**

Síle de Cléir studied Fashion Design at Limerick Technical College, working in fashion for some years before studying Folklore and Ethnology at University College, Cork. She lectures at the University of Limerick. Publications include "Ireland" in the *Berg Encyclopedia of World Dress and Fashion* (2010) and "Ritual and the City Context: Limerick 1925–1960" in *Béascna: Journal of Folklore and Ethnology* (2010).
sile.decleir@ul.ie

## Abstract

Ireland has undergone significant economic changes in the last 170 years: from the destitution of the Great Famine of the 1840s to the affluence of the Celtic Tiger years at the end of the twentieth century. This article examines the relationship of Irish people with fashion, whether as producers of crafted textiles for export to larger centers of culture in the nineteenth century, or as consumers who integrated elements of fashion with folk dress traditions. The effect of Ireland's heritage of folk material culture on the discourse of dress in the cultural nationalism of the early twentieth century is explained. The early flowering of fashion

**design in Dublin and the international success of designers such as Sybil Connolly and Irene Gilbert is discussed through the use of classic histories of Irish fashion: the subsequent performance of the industry in the freer trade environment of the 1970s and 1980s is assessed. Irish fashion today is building an international profile, while the industry copes with the challenges of multinational retailing and globalization of production. The article concludes by looking at localized fashion discourses, where groups use ritualized display to build a local engagement with the international aesthetic discourse of fashion.**

**KEYWORDS: Ireland, fashion design, identity, textiles, wool**

Assessing the changing importance of smaller countries and their cities in the global fashion environment of the twenty-first century involves an examination not just of the processes involved but also of the various actors in these processes and the relationships between them. In Ireland's case the historical process by which a rich heritage of wool and linen textiles was adapted to high fashion markets from the 1950s is central to this story, while the relationship between Irish people's changing identity and the aesthetic discourse of international fashion is the one on which it turns. Ireland's marginal position and unique history in Western Europe, its strong cultural ties to the USA, as well as its proximity to the economic power of Great Britain and to London fashion have all been important elements in how Irish fashion sees itself and relates to the rest of the world.

In this article I will look at how the history of the country has affected Ireland's relationship with fashion, clothing, and textiles, on aesthetic and practical levels. I will also examine aspects of the production and consumption of fashion in Ireland and, through government and trade reports as well as sources within the popular media, attempt to assess the country's position with regard to fashion as both an economic activity and an aspect of culture in people's lives in Ireland today.

The history of the clothing industry in Ireland must be seen first and foremost as a history of textiles, as distinctive versions of both wool and linen fabric formed the basis for the uniquely Irish styles of dress worn by members of the Gaelic aristocracy and Irish people in general as late as the seventeenth century (McClintock 1950). The quality of these fabrics—and especially wool—was the main factor in the development of well-known export products such as the heavy woolen mantle from the seventeenth century and later, in the nineteenth century, the "Ulster" overcoat (McCrum 1996: 3–4). The emphasis on quality textiles was to continue to define Ireland's export as craft products such as crochet and tambour lace were produced later in the nineteenth century, to be followed by hand-knitted sweaters in the twentieth century (McCrum 1996: 5–13). Meanwhile, a sense of fashion can be traced back to the sixteenth century in Ireland, when the highly ornate silks and velvets worn by Tudor royalty in London began to be seen among the Gaelic chieftains and their wives (Dunlevy 1989: 44–5). As the centuries progressed increasing contact with England, Scotland, and later the USA through emigration, along with an improved communications infrastructure within Ireland ensured an increasing visibility of fashion in most areas of the country. Studies by both Mairead Dunlevy and Linda-May Ballard have demonstrated the popularity of fashionable fabrics and styles among ordinary people, while research into folk dress has shown that fashionable elements were sometimes integrated with traditional styles (Ballard 2000: 62–70; de Cléir 2002: 91–2; Dunlevy 1989: 162–9). The beginnings of a fashion industry came in the 1950s when Dublin designers such as Irene Gilbert and Sybil Connolly became prominent, with the latter achieving international recognition. One of the factors in Connolly's success was her use of Irish textiles, especially linen (O'Byrne 2000a: 20–33). Designers of the 1960s such as Neillí Mulcahy and Mary O'Donnell exploited Ireland's textile heritage to the full in their use of tweed along with crochet and knitting techniques (O'Byrne 2000a: 34–47). The opening up of markets in the 1970s and 1980s, along with international developments in both textile and clothing manufacturing technology brought new challenges to the Irish fashion industry. Increased communication and competition made it crucial for Irish design to compete on an international level: many designers such as Michael Mortell and Paul Costelloe did so, while the investment in technology by clothing factories increased their efficiency and competitiveness in the 1980s (O'Byrne 2000a: 74–127). During the 1990s the business environment took on global aspects, and these have increased steadily since then. The Irish economy lost competitiveness in the first decade of the new century (Irish Clothing and Textile Alliance (ICATA) 2005). This has led to a reevaluation of the industry, which is seen as design-led with a new emphasis on outsourcing the manufacturing of garments and accessories. Design education, along with training in the management of the supply chain, in general is seen as crucial to the future of the fashion industry in Ireland today (ICATA 2010).

## Dress, Identity, and Creativity

In any discussion such as this is useful to see people as both makers and consumers of fashion: it is, however, essential in the Irish context to sometimes see these as two distinct levels of analysis. For example, clothing factory workers assembling Sybil Connolly's extravagant eveningwear in the 1950s may have been buying their own coats in the town draper's shop and making dresses for themselves from printed cotton; women in the Aran Islands in the same decade were creating bright red skirts from locally woven wool and making warm blouses from a mixture of light shop-bought wool and velvet to wear themselves, while knitting sweaters for the tourist market.

The decisions people make regarding their own dress can operate quite independently of involvement in fashion as a business, and in Ireland, for most of the twentieth century, the extent to which people's dress decisions were tied into international fashion discourse varied greatly, for both economic and aesthetic reasons. The Irish scholar of folklore and mythology, Gearóid Ó Crualaoich, has described how individuals and communities continually create "islands of identity" out of the ocean of culture flowing around them (2003: 6): in this way, aspects of global culture are meaningfully interpreted and re-created in a local communal context. This idea is particularly appropriate to dress and fashion, where international trends are reinterpreted and worn for oneself, and for family and friends, in one's own "cultural island" whether this is a country area, a town or a city. Appreciating this local aspect of fashion helps us to understand how what Lou Taylor has called "the globalised world of mass commodified international fashion" (2002: 79) is played out at local level: it also highlights the differing roles of Irish people in fashion, as creators, makers, promoters, and consumers. The evolution of these roles, the interplay between them, and their relative importance in the lives of people is a significant indicator of the state of fashion in Ireland today.

## Philanthropy and Fashion: Crochet, Lace, and Embroidery

Ireland's disastrous material situation in the mid-nineteenth century—which reached its crisis in the Great Famine of the late 1840s—was unusual, if not unique in Western European terms, and made all the worse by the country's proximity to the economic powerhouse of the British Empire (Ó Gráda 1999). Poverty and deprivation in Ireland was a cause for concern throughout the nineteenth century and led to various initiatives to stimulate the economy and give employment to people. Textile crafts played an important part in these initiatives: lacemaking was one of the most important, with the Limerick and Carrickmacross schools becoming the best known as the century progressed (Ó Cléirigh and Rowe 1995). Crochet lace, introduced in Cork in the post-Famine period, was also significant (McCrum 1996: 11). These high-profile locations were just some of the lace schools in a countrywide network that developed over the second half of the nineteenth century (Shaw-Smith 1984: 42–3). The increasing importance of lace and other crafted textiles in fashionable dress from the 1890s gave impetus to the efforts of philanthropists such as Alice Rowland Hart and Ishbel, Countess of Aberdeen. The former set up the Donegal Industrial Fund and sold Irish-crafted goods through her retail outlet in London from the mid-1880s (Helland 2007: 24–75). The latter founded the Irish Industries

Association and recruited other high-profile patrons to help and continue the work of promoting and selling not just lace but Irish fabrics, such as linen, wool, and silk poplin, which was being woven in Dublin at the time. Aberdeen's promotional activities included organizing a Vice-Regal Garden Party for Dublin's elite in 1886, at which the wearing of Irish clothing was required. She also ensured the participation of Irish home arts and cottage crafts at international exhibitions, such as that held in Edinburgh in 1886 and, most notably, at the Chicago World's Fair in 1893, at which a special "Irish Village" was constructed, with lacemakers, spinners, and knitters brought from Ireland especially for the occasion (Helland 2007: 76–142). Hart and Aberdeen were just two of many philanthropist-entrepreneurs who succeeded in using and developing further the already considerable textile skills of the female population and linking these to the world of fashionable dress. The emphasis on fine textiles in fashion from the late 1880s to the period just before the First World War was a key factor in their success. The exhibition in Chicago was of particular importance, not just because of the sheer numbers of people who viewed the Irish textiles there, but because of Lady Aberdeen's decision to hand over the management of the "Irish village" to a newly arrived Dublin woman named Annie White, whose daughter, Carmel—then just six years old—would later become the highly influential editor-in-chief of *Harper's Bazaar* from 1934 to 1958 (Rowlands 2005: 12–16). Thus was the scene set for an association of Ireland not just with high quality textile crafts, but also with the world of international high fashion as the twentieth century progressed.

## Dress and National Identity

It is useful here, too, to look at the part played by dress in the formation of a sense of national identity from the late nineteenth century to the middle of the twentieth, a sixty-year period that was marked by great political and social change. Hilary O'Kelly's research on the styles of dress adopted by cultural nationalists in the period between 1880 and 1920 shows how various "niche" groups within the revival movement handled the question of dress: she describes:

> Women who were attached to the Abbey Theatre ... walking through Dublin in long dresses and flowing cloaks ... their costumes were not particularly Irish except in the fancy Celtic fixtures attached, but they enjoyed the symbolism and romanticism of the costumes which brought them into line with European artistic movements. (O'Kelly 1992: 82)

O'Kelly also mentions the work of the Dún Emer Guild, set up "in an Arts and Crafts spirit" by the Yeats sisters. Here, the pre-Norman garments of *brat* (a cloak) and *léine* (a longish tunic) were made in Irish silk poplin, embroidered with Celtic designs worked in bright colors (O'Kelly 1992: 82). However, Mairead Dunlevy's work shows that the Guild also produced fashionable dresses adorned with similar embroideries (Dunlevy 1989: 177). Speaking of Irish revivalists generally, O'Kelly says: "For the vast majority of the Gaelic League, Irish dress was interpreted as being fashionable dress made of Irish fabrics" (O'Kelly 1992: 77). O'Kelly also comments that, even among the most dedicated dress revivalists, "The 'Irish Costume' never became a strict uniform" (O'Kelly 1992: 82).

The best extant example of traditional dress in these years, and in the early decades of the Irish Free State, was to be found in the Aran Islands, and even here the links to fashion were considerable: fine patterned cottons and shop-bought velvets for blouse-making, and, in later years, shoulder shawls crocheted from brightly colored bought yarn are two examples, while the overall fashion literacy of the community is demonstrated by the differing sets of clothes—one traditional, another fashionable—owned by many women (de Cléir 2002: 91). The crucial link between Irish textile crafts and the world of fashion is highlighted by the speed at which the distinctive Aran sweater with its richly patterned allover texture was adopted and developed for an international craft and fashion market in the 1930s and 1940s (O'Byrne 2000a: 131).

The dynamic relationship between folk dress and fashion meant that these two areas were seen as aesthetically and culturally complementary rather than oppositional to one another, while Ireland's relative paucity of artifacts ensured that static forms of traditional dress did not acquire symbolic importance in the discourse of nationality. The continued focus on fabrics and crafts *co-ordinated* with fashion—rather than the isolation of fossilized forms of "peasant dress" that were then regarded as a "national costume"—meant that folk and fashionable dress were not regarded as mutually exclusive but rather that the use of folk crafts in fashion was seen by many as a key part of the progress of Irish fashion design as it began to evolve in the middle of the twentieth century.

## Dublin's Moment: The 1950s and 1960s

Ireland's proximity to London as well as the historical relationship between the two countries were significant factors—but not the only ones—in the view of Ireland as a producer of quality fabrics and textile crafts rather than as a center of design in the first half of the twentieth century. Robert O'Byrne's account shows that Irish-born designers such as Edward Molyneux, Digby Morton, and John Cavanagh chose not to base themselves in Dublin or in any part of Ireland, but to go to London (or Paris, in the case of Edward Molyneux), and work there instead (O'Byrne 2000a: 15–16). Where clothing manufacturing existed, it was concentrated on reproducing international fashion trends in quality Irish fabrics and selling them to a mostly domestic market, in economic conditions made favorable by tariffs on imported goods (O'Byrne 2000a: 18). Culturally, the emphasis on buying Irish goods, along with an appreciation of the superior quality of Irish fabrics, was of great importance in the decades following Irish independence.[1] Dressmaking and tailoring—where clothing is made for individuals rather than manufactured in large quantities—were also significant elements of the economy in the cities and towns of Ireland (Clear 2008: 76).

Yet there is a qualitative difference between being a dressmaker—however upmarket—and being a fashion designer, and in the context of Dublin, and Ireland generally, it is worth exploring where this difference lies. A sense of originality or creativity in design is perhaps the most important characteristic of the work of someone who sees themselves as a designer rather than simply as a dressmaker: a designer's perception of themselves and their work must also be conveyed to others who understand and appreciate what the designer is trying to create, or "say." In this sense, the fashion show could be seen as a self-conscious exercise in communication of the designer's vision, as well as a practical marketing strategy. The fashion show event depends on the designer and the public having a common understanding of the discourse of fashion at that moment, with the designer re-creating and interpreting current trends. Because of this, the fashion show held by hat designer Irene Gilbert in Jammet's Restaurant in Dublin in 1950 (O'Byrne 2000a: 23) could be seen as significant: in this event we see not just the designer's perception of herself as a creative artist with something interesting to show, but also her understanding that there were enough fashion-conscious people in Dublin at that time to appreciate her work. Valerie Steele, in her discussion of Paris as a center of fashion, notes the existence there of a cosmopolitan society where "ritualized fashion display" was welcomed (Steele 1988: 285). Though it would be difficult to characterize 1950s Dublin, in general, as "cosmopolitan"—and of course Steele is referring to rituals in a wider sense than that of the fashion show—Gilbert's staging of a show does indicate the existence of a cohort of people who were interested in and stimulated by the event. The location of the show was also significant, in an urban sense: Jammet's, an upmarket restaurant, was also an important gathering place for writers and artists in the city, a popular venue for special literary or artistic dinners, and a world away from the aristocratic displays of textile crafts and clothing held in the splendor of the Vice-Regal Lodge or in the homes of titled ladies such as Ishbel Aberdeen in the late nineteenth century (Fallon 1998: 153). The sense of a creative, artistic urban environment for the display of clothing—rather than simply a high-class one—is to be felt in Gilbert's choice of venue. It is important to note that this link between clothing and creativity was not new in Dublin, which had had an academy of dress design since the late 1930s (McCrum 1996: 83; O'Byrne 2000a: 49). It is possible too that Gilbert's fashion show was not the first held in Dublin, but her subsequent success and consistent emphasis on showing her designs both in Ireland and internationally demonstrates her appreciation of herself as a designer, and of the importance of at least one aspect of "ritualized fashion display" in the promotion of a designer's work.

After her first fashion show, Irene Gilbert expanded into clothing design, and became what Elizabeth McCrum has described as "one of the traditional perfectionist couturiers," showing her first full collection in 1951. She worked closely with textile companies, making creative use of Irish woolen and linen fabrics, but not limiting herself to these. Gilbert is noteworthy because of this: her designs ranged from beautifully tailored tweed suits with coordinating items crafted from the same yarn to draped or bias-cut evening dresses in softer, clinging (sometimes synthetic) fabrics.

Her feeling for fashion was also unerring, as her collections produced through the 1960s show. By this time, Gilbert was producing ready-to-wear clothing, much of it for export to the USA and Canada. Her high-profile clients included the Irish-American Princess Grace of Monaco, for whom she made an evening dress of Carrickmacross lace, and Anne, Countess of Rosse, who was an enthusiastic supporter of Irish designers both at home and abroad (McCrum 1996: 18–20). Figure 1 shows a photograph by Richard Dormer of a tweed suit by Irene Gilbert that appeared in *Harper's Bazaar* in 1954. Gilbert's love of Irish fabric, along with her strong instinct for trends make this an individual, but fashion-forward look, while the pose of the model—who is almost, but not quite smoking—gives the image a sophisticated edge.

The best-known Irish designer of the 1950s was undoubtedly Sybil Connolly, who had started her career working for Dublin clothing manufacturer and retailer Jack Clarke in the early 1940s. Clarke launched his upmarket label Country Wear in 1944, and employed a French-Canadian designer, Gaston Mallet, in 1949. When Mallet left in 1952 Connolly took over, designing a couture line with her own Sybil Connolly label, along with Clarke's other lines (O'Byrne 2000a: 26–7).

Sybil Connolly was noted for her love of Irish fabrics and crafts. She used the red flannel associated with traditional dress for long evening skirts and dramatic cloaks; she used tweeds for boldly tailored swing jackets and flamboyant coats; she used fine woolen fabric for voluminous pleated dresses with cinched waists. She used Irish crochet lace for blouses and, most notably, she used finely pleated handkerchief linen to make romantic evening dresses, blouses, and skirts. It took eight meters of this fine linen to make one meter of pleated cloth, which was reputed to be uncrushable (McCrum 1996: 15–18; O'Byrne 2000b: 109–119).

Connolly initially benefited from a clothing export environment in which the government played a supportive role, and from North American networks already used by the highly successful Jack Clarke, whom

**Figure 1**
Irish fashion in Irish fabric: a suit by Irene Gilbert, photographed by Richard Dormer and featured in *Harper's Bazaar*, 1954. Image courtesy of the National Magazine Company.

Elizabeth McCrum describes as "the trailblazer for the whole Irish clothing export trade" (McCrum 1996: 15). In a significant move for Irish fashion, Córas Tráchtála Teoranta (The Irish Export Board) brought the Philadelphia Fashion Group to Dublin to see Connolly's collection in 1952 (McCrum 1996: 16). As a result of this, and the press coverage gained from it, she was invited to show in some American stores for the Spring/Summer 1953 season. It was around this time too, that Connolly came to the attention of the dynamic and innovative Carmel Snow, who had been editor of *Harper's Bazaar* in New York since 1934. Penelope Rowlands describes how Snow came to Dublin in July 1953, with a group of fashion journalists and buyers. Connolly's collection was shown in the romantic setting of Dunsany Castle, and was photographed by Richard Avedon for the October edition of *Harper's Bazaar*. Accounts of this period agree that Carmel Snow had a significant role in promoting Connolly's work in the USA from this time on. She described herself as loving Connolly's "charming use of Irish tweeds and muslins" while *Vogue* writer Bettina Ballard said that the designer "bewitched us all into buying her models and filling our editorial pages with them" (Rowlands 2005: 443–5). In Fall 1953, Sybil Connolly was pictured on the cover of *Life* magazine, with the headline "Irish Invade Fashion World," and was featured in many other American publications. From then on, the designer returned to the USA twice a year, showing her collections in many different cities and stores. Her clients came to include Jacqueline Kennedy and Elizabeth Taylor (Rowlands 2005: 446).

It is important to appreciate the significance of Connolly's success for Irish fashion in general during this time. Elizabeth McCrum has the following to say: "It was during this period, in the mid-1950s, that buyers and journalists who visited France, England and Italy every season added Ireland to their itinerary" (McCrum 1996: 16). In a footnote, McCrum tells us that the March 1956 cover of *Harper's Bazaar* had printed on its cover: "Spring collections Paris London Dublin Italy" (McCrum 1996: 138) while Robert O'Byrne comments, "I do dearly love those covers of *Harper's Bazaar* and *Vogue* from the 1950s, on which Dublin is ranked as a equal player with London and Paris" (O'Byrne 2000a: 7).

Throughout the 1950s and1960s, other Irish designers were to benefit from the international attention garnered by Connolly. These would include Neillí Mulcahy and Mary O'Donnell, both of whom interpreted current trends using Irish fabrics and craft techniques to a large extent (O'Byrne 2000a: 37–44). Clodagh O'Kennedy has described her own design style in the 1960s as "luxurious minimalism"—figure-hugging crochet dresses and fine tweed cut in a simple, modern style (O'Byrne 2000a: 44–6). The work of these designers—and many other Irish designers at the time—was boosted not just by the continued support of government agencies but also by the interest in their work and the support of it among the Irish diaspora in the USA and in Britain (McCrum 1996: 32–3). Robert O'Byrne has pointed out that from a purely economic point of view, the British market was far more significant, in export terms, than the American market in the 1950s and 1960s (O'Byrne 2000a: 35), but it must be said that the profile of Irish fashion was high and the sense of Dublin as a center of fashion design was strong, in both Britain and America, during this period.

## A Time of Transition: 1970–2000

Ireland's entry into the European Economic Community in 1973 led to a situation where free trade was brought in on a phased basis as the decade progressed (Haughton 2008: 22). Changes in fashion and advances in fabric technology along with a changed aesthetic of dress among younger people brought significant challenges to the clothing industry in Ireland. In retrospect, Irish designers and manufacturers can be seen to have risen to this challenge.

Designer Pat Crowley, who had worked with Irene Gilbert in the 1960s, continued the tradition of Irish women *couturières* producing feminine clothes featuring a high concentration of crafted techniques (McCrum 1996: 38–41). Thomas Wolfangel was renowned for his superb tailoring in Irish and other woolen fabrics; the young Richard Lewis was distinguishing himself through his sensual use of matt jersey in day- and eveningwear (O'Byrne 2000a: 54–5; 59–61). Ib Jorgensen, also at couture level, produced elegant grown-up clothes sometimes featuring painted or embroidered fabrics produced by his wife, textile designer Patricia Jorgensen (McCrum 1996: 41). In this decade too, and in the 1980s, Irish labels operating at the mid to upmarket had considerable success in ready-to-wear, with trouser suits and other tailored ensembles in light wool—much of it Irish—and in other fabrics selling well in the home and export markets. The Michael Jacobs label designed by Peter Fitzsimons and the work of designer Patrick Howard were of considerable importance in this regard (O'Byrne 2000a: 76–83). Figure 2 shows a typical Patrick Howard ensemble. The image of this label as a high-quality, fashionable range, designed and manufactured in Ireland, was a crucial factor in its success among young professional women in the 1970s. The Loretta Bloom label, founded in the early 1980s, was noted at the time for its investment in manufacturing technology, and produced beautifully tailored coordinates from its factory in Limerick

**Figure 2**
Making it work: Patrick Howard's suit in fine Irish herringbone tweed, 1980, photographed by Neil Campbell-Sharp and featured in *IT* (*Irish Tatler*) magazine. Image courtesy of Neil Campbell-Sharp.

for the domestic and export markets. Two Irish fashion magazines of the 1970s, *Image*, founded in 1973, and *Irish Tatler* (or *IT*)—originally founded in 1890 as *Irish Tatler and Sketch*—played a significant role in showcasing Irish fashion, with the latter particularly dedicated to this (O'Byrne 2000a: 74).

The early 1980s saw efforts to consolidate and strengthen the industry against a constantly changing manufacturing and retailing landscape both in Ireland and internationally: the varying success of these initiatives is to some extent indicative of the pressure and mixed priorities within the sector at the time. Irish Fashion Week, instance, founded to showcase designers at the upper end of the market, ran for a few years in the 1980s, but was not financially viable in the long-term. The need to establish a retail outlet in a prestigious location where a number of Irish designers' work could be seen together was something upon which all were agreed, however, and the Design Centre, founded in 1984 in Dublin, is still flourishing (O'Byrne 2000a: 87–8).

In discussing the 1970s and early 1980s, Patrick Howard has pointed out that "there were far fewer of us around and you didn't have the big machines like Dunnes Stores producing wonderful clothes and selling them very well" (O'Byrne 2000a: 80). It is certainly true that as the 1980s progressed, the mass-market retail scene was changing in significant ways, especially in terms of the design and cut of its products, while the quality and variety of inexpensive fabrics available to designers and manufacturers of budget clothing was constantly improving. Robert O'Byrne has pointed out that Ireland's boom that began in the mid-1990s exacerbated this situation as far as the Irish clothing industry was concerned (O'Byrne 2000a: 156): whereas Britain had always been Ireland's most valuable export market, major British retailers such as Marks and Spencer and Next now began to see Ireland as a lucrative retailing location. This combined with an almost feverish approach to property development of all kinds—including shopping malls—at the end of the twentieth century, meant that giant multinational clothing retailers of many nationalities established a presence in all the Irish cities as well as in some of the large towns. As Irish people were perceived as more affluent, upmarket department stores such as the Brown Thomas group were stocking more and more international design names, who now also saw Ireland as a potential market, but whose marketing and operations budgets were far more substantial than their Irish equivalents.

A 2005 report commissioned by the Irish Clothing and Textile Alliance outlines the effect not just of the changed retailing scene but of other aspects of the Celtic Tiger economy on the industry:

> The long-term trend decline in output in the textiles and clothing sector continued in 2005, reflecting the increasing importance of outsourcing. Ireland is now a high-cost country not only in

> terms of labour costs but in all of the non-wage business costs ... (ICATA 2005: 1)

This report showed significant increases in retail sales of textiles and clothing but steady decreases in both output and employment in the sector. Between 1990 and 2005, output decreased by 75 percent (ICATA 2005: 1). In 1995, the industry employed just under 20,000 people; in 2005 that had fallen to 4,975 (ICATA 2005: 2). The sense of loss in the closure of a factory is palpable in the comment from Libra Designs, whose website states that "Our much more humble beginnings as a blouse manufacturer under the Libra label have become a remote but treasured memory" (Libra Designs 2009). Libra is a company that has successfully managed the transition from manufacturing to design and outsourcing: the Loretta Bloom company, which was liquidated in 2004, did not fare as well. The loss of this business, located in the clothing district of Limerick city where factories with several hundreds of employees had operated since the mid-nineteenth century, could be seen as particularly poignant and symbolic of the decline of the industry in the country in general.

## Relocation and Recovery: Fashion in Ireland Now

The business of fashion in Ireland as we enter the second decade of the century is many-faceted. Two examples of long-established, internationally successful designers are Paul Costelloe and John Rocha (O'Byrne 2000a: 83–5; 95–6; 121–3).[2] Both could be said to have to have employed aspects of Irishness in their design aesthetic: Costelloe through his use of natural materials and sense of muted understatement; Rocha through his love of rich textures and surface embellishment. Louise Kennedy's long-term success has not depended on ethnic aspects such as these, but on elegance, wearability, and impeccable tailoring (O'Byrne 2000a: 125–7). All of these designers have begun to design ranges of homewares as part of their businesses. Lainey Keogh is a knitwear designer whose sustained international success is not surprising given her dramatic, sometimes romantic, designs and her adventurous approach to yarn and technique (O'Byrne 2000a: 137–41). The long-term success of the Quin and Donnelly label is founded on their on-trend but wearable clothes in high-quality fabrics and exciting colors (O'Byrne 2000a: 88–90). More recently established designers include Joanne Hynes, whose look is edgy in a very feminine way, and Lucy Downes, who makes casually elegant knitwear in cashmere under the Sphere One label. The above are just some of the successful designers operating in Ireland: the fact that two of them are knitwear designers is not surprising given the long-term popularity of knitwear, the craft element involved, and the way this resonates with people's notions of quality. Anne Melinn, a lecturer in Fashion Design at the Limerick Institute of Technology has said:

> Knitwear is still of huge importance and in a recession it is always the bestseller ... We have come full circle in that there is a turn back to craft and even handknitting. You also have the huge eco-friendly possibilities opened up by recycled yarn. (Anne Melinn, personal communication, April 19, 2010)

The production of knitwear varies from the outsourcing model used by Lucy Downes, whose garments are produced in Nepal, to the workshop approach operated, for example, by Limerick designer Caroline Mitchell. Knitwear factories still operate quite successfully in Ireland; the Carraig Donn factory in Westport and Inis Meáin Knitwear, located on one of the Aran Islands, are two examples.

The need for Irish design to compete in an ever-more global fashion industry was the inspiration behind the first significant initiative since the 1980s to bring Irish designers' work together and promote it effectively: Dublin Fashion Week (DFW) was founded in 2005 with the aim of showcasing 25–30 Irish designers twice a year. The relatively small number of labels showing along with the location of the show in Dublin is, according to its director, Sonia Reynolds, an advantage for the designers and a point of interest for international buyers: "If designers go to bigger centres they are a small fish in a big pond. It's not Paris, London or New York but more of a 'boutique' idea—like Copenhagen." (Sonia Reynolds, personal communication, April 15, 2010). Reynolds cites the financial support of the Dublin City Enterprise Board as being important, but also that of retailer Brown Thomas, who sponsored the event for some years. Brown Thomas also provided a mentoring service to young designers through the event, leading, in the case of Joanne Hynes, to a concession within the Dublin store. Reynolds also describes the businesslike or "trade" orientation of DFW:

> It's all about real selling ... designers, samples, and selling. Buyers seeing the designers at their full capacity. DFW is about a package—product, marketing and press. Irish designers are competing with international labels—Dutch, Belgian, Italian. The product has to be right, and the price. (Personal communication)

The sense that the promotion of Irish designers is perceived as economically and culturally important is borne out by the strong support given to DFW by the press. The idea that local designers might have something interesting to offer is to be found at consumer level as well: Aisling Kilduff, director of the Design Centre—which now stocks international labels as well—has recently said:

> My customers always appreciated Irish design ... but this past year, customers are coming in and the first thing they ask me is:

> "Where are the Irish labels?" and the fact is, they are now nearly the whole store, such is the demand. (Harris 2010)

Regular coverage of Irish designers' work in the national press bolsters the profile of Irish designers and stimulates curiosity about them and their work. The *Irish Times* newspaper, for instance, over a two-month period in 2010, featured the work of Joanne Hynes in its January pages (McQuillan 2010a); in February it profiled Ruth Duignan, Heidi Higgins, Eilish Kennedy, and Mia O'Connell in one three-page spread (McQuillan 2010b); while later in the same month the magazine cover and a two-page feature inside showed Úna Burke's "extraordinary leather pieces, which explore the effect of trauma on the human body and mind" while noting that the singer Lady Gaga has commissioned some of Burke's work (McQuillan 2010c).

The creativity of these designers and the individuality of their work are in contrast to the world of fast fashion where the mass production of ever-cheaper clothes has intensified in the last ten years. The Primark label, trading in Ireland as Penney's, is a good example of this. Founded in Dublin in 1969, the company is now British-owned, but retains a strong presence and identity in Ireland through its thirty-eight Irish stores. The group's international profile is high, with outlets in Britain, Spain, the Netherlands, Portugal, Germany, Belgium, and Holland. If any company has managed to embrace the outsourcing model and streamline its supply chain—and thus compete in a global context—it is this one. Yet Primark is not lauded for its success, and is not claimed as an "originally Irish" success story. This is partly because of the loss of individuality brought about by such major expansion, but it is also related to a sense of uncertainty and unease around the issue of how the clothes are produced. An article entitled "The True Cost of Low Prices" in the *Irish Times* in January 2010 stated that

> In 2006, Primark was rocked by the War on Want campaign's "Fashion Victims" report, revealing that garment workers in Bangladesh worked in appalling conditions for up to 80 hours a week, in violation of local law. (Scally 2010)

Since then, the company has set up an ethical trade division to monitor conditions in the factories it uses. While campaigners claim that improvements are slow in coming, Primark's Breege O'Donoghue points out that many other, more expensive labels outsource their manufacturing to factories such as these:

> Irrespective of what (price) is on the label, the workers are paid the same ... our factories are shared by 98.3 per cent of our competitors ... Clearly in the market place we're in there's a

> market rate for production. That's the kind of business we're in. (Scally 2010)

It is this "kind of business" that makes people, however much they may love to buy clothes at competitive prices, or beautifully made clothes by an Irish designer, uncomfortable about the globalization of the clothing industry at all levels of the market. The organization of Dublin Ethical Fashion Week—now in its third year—reflects a growing concern about the human ethical aspect of fashion among the media and the fashion public. The fact that many garment-makers no longer display a country of manufacture on the label exacerbates this problem. Even while the reports of government agencies and sectoral interest groups are recommending outsourcing, and "servicisation" of industry (Intertrade Ireland 2000: 21) this is a topic that, at point of sale, is quietly ignored for the most part.[3] The Irish designers who assure their customers of the ethical trading conditions of their operations are few and far between, though it may well be that in many cases employment practices are fair and local labor laws are respected. Thus, while all are agreed that Irish fashion should survive and succeed, the question of just how Irish designers are surviving and succeeding is more difficult. The marketing strategies of fashion itself make this question even more complex, as Dublin couturier Peter O'Brien explains:

> There was a time when designers made expensive clothes for women with lots of money to buy them. Nowadays the expensive clothes you see on TV and on the runways are only advertising campaigns for handbags and perfume. If you don't have these commodities it can be very difficult to make money. (O'Brien 2005)

This comment highlights how the fashion system demands that as designers' businesses grow, making clothes becomes less important than running a franchising empire. For the buying public, virtual fashion is everywhere and an awareness of trends in the major centers is very high, while the end products of the process are easily obtained. Yet, even as more and more people participate in the visual and material discourse of fashion, there are signs of fatigue with the constant hype and the loss of authenticity that this brings about. Sonia Reynolds's idea that international buyers, having seen the hundreds of designers in London Fashion Week, might come to Dublin for a more "boutique" and individual experience is reminiscent of the spirit in which Carmel Snow led her troupe of buyers and journalists to Dublin in the 1950s. For a much more fashion-aware Irish public, there are signs too of a desire for a somewhat more authentic fashion experience than that offered by multinational retail chains in shopping malls. Limerick Institute of Technology fashion design lecturer Anne Melinn says:

> The boutique element is very important—personal shopping, the charm of being attended to properly, the idea of shopping as an occasion and a "day out". The idea of going to peculiar places to get something a bit different—all this has opened up. (Personal communication)

The growth in importance of independent boutiques not just in cities but in small towns in Ireland is evidence of this; these range from large, multi-floor stores with excellent personal service selling in the mid- to upmarket range, to smaller boutiques selling highly individual pieces by Irish and international designers. The owners' knowledge not just of the labels they stock but of their customers and of their individual needs and tastes are important factors in the success of these smaller shops.[4] Deirdre Devaney, the fashion director of Dublin store Arnotts, has recently highlighted the importance of local awareness in fashion retailing, saying:

> You can't give black away in Cork. It is a really different look there—everybody loves colour and black is for funerals. In Galway, they love dressing up and you really see it at the taxi ranks during the Galway races. There's a great sense of style in Limerick and some great boutiques outside the city. That's why UK multiples get it wrong. Each of our regions has to be treated differently and that's what gives us the edge. (McQuillan: 2010d)

The sense of the value of a more individual, local experience is also in evidence in the organization of fashion shows and "fashion weeks" in smaller cities and country areas. Though these are perhaps more "lifestyle" events aimed mainly at the end customer, the fact that many designers participate in them is testament to their importance and potential usefulness to them, whether in garnering individual couture clients, or in promoting manufactured ranges of clothing and accessories. They also operate as a form of "ritualised fashion display" for the area, making it a center of fashion, even if only in a temporary sense, as the promotion for one of these events in 2008 illustrates: "Move over London ... introducing Galway Fashion Week" (Regan 2008).

Kerry Fashion Weekend, held in 2009 and 2010, was promoted in a similar way. The county of Kerry—affectionately nicknamed "The Kingdom" in sporting and other cultural contexts—was dubbed "The Kingdom of Style" and, as one journalist put it: "We know it's not Paris or Milan Fashion Week but remember the devil is not always in Prada—it's in the detail. And in the style and *joie de vivre*" (Egan 2009). As part of this event, Kerry had its Designer of the Year awards with Louise Kennedy and Melanie Morris, editor of *Image* magazine, among the judges. The palpable sense of place inherent in the Galway and Kerry fashion events is strengthened by the fact that both are areas of great natural beauty with thriving tourist industries. The connections between fashion and lifestyle events and local retailing is clear from the Cork Fashion Week 2010 schedule, which included, as one of its highlights, a "Boutique Show." Dublin city, on the other hand, is focused on international trade and is unquestionably the only urban area in Ireland that sees itself in this role. The change of name from the more general "Irish Fashion Week" of the 1980s to "Dublin Fashion Week" promotes the city as a center of fashion while still implying a sense of individuality in that global discourse; this tight geographical and commercial focus is also useful in terms of sponsorship from local government agencies and city retailers.

## By Way of Conclusion ...

In terms of how we look at Ireland's status as a center of fashion, it is worth briefly revisiting the 1950s when the international spotlight hovered over Dublin for a number of years. Ireland, at this point, would seem to have had many of the characteristics of a "fashion nation": designers producing collections which were both recognizably "Irish" but also aesthetically exciting from a fashion perspective; a clothing industry employing significant numbers of people and strongly supported by the government; a public who were reasonably fashion-aware; and a labor force highly skilled in the area of textiles and clothing. It must be remembered also that the sense of Ireland as a new state and the hope and idealism engendered by this was a factor in both the official attitude to the clothing industry and the international view of Irish design. However, the cyclical nature of fashion meant that the tweeds and linens of the 1950s, along with the flamboyant romanticism of the Irish look at that time, fell out of favor in the 1960s. Sybil Connolly, who had capitalized most on this, declared herself at odds with fashion at the end of the 1960s, and her collections, though still bought by faithful clients, were not as highly regarded as previously (O'Byrne 2000b: 114).

Irene Gilbert, though not as well known, managed to combine a love of Irish fibers and fabrics and an ethnic aesthetic with a strong instinct for fashion and an openness to newer materials and creative technology. This is what Paul Costelloe, John Rocha, Lainey Keogh, and companies such as Inis Meáin knitwear have succeeded in doing in recent years, and, though not as dramatic as Connolly's approach, it seems a better formula for long-term recognition. Figure 3 shows a John Rocha ensemble for Spring 2010. In an interesting departure from his usual monochrome palette, Rocha's bright red skirt with textural interest around its circumference is reminiscent of the traditional *cóta* of the Aran Islanders' dress in the early twentieth century, while still retaining a light, contemporary, and fashionable quality.

**Figure 3**
Contemporary classic: John Rocha, 2010. Photographed by Andreas Pettersson and featured in *Sunday Independent—Life* magazine. Image courtesy of Andreas Pettersson.

In terms of Irish people, how they dress themselves, and how they experience fashion and build their own "islands of identity" through dress, in retrospect most would not nowadays regard the 1950s as a "golden age": it was an era when deprivation was common and poverty a constant threat to many, though it should be noted that this did not prevent women from having an interest in their appearance and engaging with fashion, as Caitriona Clear's research shows (2008). It was also a decade of economic stagnation and high emigration. As Robert O'Byrne has pointed out, Connolly's success in America was built on the relatively low prices of her highly crafted garments, a fact made possible by low labor costs for all kinds of textile production as well as for cutting and garment assembly in factories in Ireland at the time (Haughton 2008: 20; O'Byrne 2000a: 31). This indicates an economic disparity between producers and consumers of clothing, something that can be found in many eras and contexts of the history of fashion. Irish people nowadays are better equipped, even in the economic recession, to follow fashion, to enjoy its aesthetic aspects, and to play with them in creative ways. The ongoing and increasing popularity of fashion design courses is testament to this. Design lecturer Anne Melinn argues that for design students, working in relative isolation from the major fashion centers serves to intensify creativity and innovation, a fact she feels is borne out by the consistent success of Limerick Institute of Technology students in seeking international work placements on the basis of their design portfolios. For the ordinary person, as well as for those working in fashion, the availability of fast fashion and the global aspects of fashion discourse are taken for granted: yet I think that the situation with local "fashion weeks" and independent boutiques shows that people will, within the tidal wave of fashionable discourse, use local networks to build their own "islands of identity" and use these as bases for engaging with the grand narrative.

## Perspectives on Irish Fashion Communities

The situation with Irish fashion magazines is also interesting.[5] The longstanding upmarket glossy *Image* has been on the shelves now for nearly forty years. The middle-market glossies, *Irish Tatler* and *U*, were, in 2004, at the height of the economic boom, challenged by a title called *Prudence*, which, ironically for a fashion magazine, advised readers on how to save money in "Rip Off Ireland" while still being stylish: *Prudence*, a bimonthly, now styles itself "Ireland's most recession-relevant magazine." More interesting still, perhaps, is the regionalization of magazines: since 2001, three monthly fashion glossies, *Cork Now*, *Limerick Now*, and *Galway Now* have been successfully circulating in the south, midwest, and western areas of the country. The same trend can be seen in the celebrity magazines, arguably an important site of ritualized fashion display for many people. The English edition of *Hello!* Magazine first went on sale in Ireland in the late 1980s, followed some years later by the very similar *OK!* In 2000, an Irish celebrity magazine called *VIP* was launched and there is now a similar, but more Munster-oriented, magazine called *RSVP*, based in the southern city of Cork. These local fashion and celebrity magazines are popular and can be bought in small village shops, which would never carry any edition of *Vogue*, though they do sell *Image*, *Irish Tatler*, and *U*. In 2010 A friendly note on the title page of *RSVP* advised readers that "If a shop that you wish to purchase a copy of our magazine in does not have it in stock for you let us know and we will address it for you"—this illustrates the aspiration of the magazine to be both as local and as national as possible at the same time.

The importance of locality can also be felt among the fashion blogs, street-style blogs, and fashion chat sites on the Internet where aesthetic aspects of dress are constantly discussed by ordinary people. In this huge global arena, references to identity are frequent—beaut.ie calls itself 'the Irish beauty blog'; the local context is all too obvious in dublinstreets.blogspot.com, while stylist Annemarie O'Connor's iblogfashion.blogspot.

com is another example of the global-but-local fashion discourse. It seems that people—even though they see themselves as participating in global culture—still want to be part of some kind of smaller cultural group, in a much more local sense than the grand narrative of fashion allows.

The empowerment of small clothing businesses by the Internet is also of major significance in this regard. As an economical source of worldwide advertising, the Internet is of course invaluable, but it also opens up a flexible discursive space in which businesses can articulate their aims, ideas, and opinions. As Ireland struggles with a severe recession, more thoughtful approaches to consumption and waste along with a new concern with ethical and environmental issues in fashion have led to the emergence of businesses that challenge accepted ideas about how people clothe themselves. Epoch Boutique, in Dublin's Temple Bar sells "'... high quality vintage pieces ... designer classics, revamped clothing and accessories which have been made from recycled materials; and clothing which has been made independently and is sweatshop free" (Epoch 2009). According to its website, Epoch "is about a new era of fashion that can be frivolous and affordable without being disposable" (Epoch 2010).

The Belfast-based Fashion Souk, a regular market for recycled and hand-crafted clothes is part of a larger group of related events including the Belfast Stitch and Style workshops, which allow creators and consumers from all over Ireland to exhibit, buy or learn to customize their own clothes. According to its website, the Fashion Souk: "... celebrates the joy of dressing up or down, of difference or wearing one-offs, and of shopping for clothes while you are doing your bit for the environment and reduce waste" (Etsy Ireland 2010).

The Rediscover Fashion initiative, based in Ballymun in Dublin: "engages with the local community on global issues relating to the environmental impact of the fashion and textile industry" (Rediscovery Centre 2010). This group sells "recycled, reconstructed and repurposed clothing" online, and at fashion shows and environmental events. Unlike Epoch Boutique, Rediscover is a "not for profit" organization, funded by a mixture of government agencies and private sponsorship; the Fashion Souk has also received some degree of public funding, while still encouraging trade, enterprise, and profit. In all these cases, however, the emphasis on a new kind of creativity is to be found: this is not the hard-won globally acknowledged fashion sense that leads to diffusion lines and homeware deals with large department stores, but a more localized aesthetic excitement that is further enriched by the values it represents and by the cultural relationships in which it is embedded.

Thus we can see how, within a globalized fashion system, Ireland is participating and surviving as a center of trade, even though the production and employment in clothing and textiles is relatively small: fashion—apart from its crafted elements—is now seen as primarily a service industry where design and management are crucial to success.

Meanwhile, though elements of continuity can be discerned in the clothing business—most notably in the exceptional, deeply rooted confidence around knitwear design and manufacturing—for the most part, Irish people's view of themselves in relation to fashion has undergone dramatic changes. No longer simply makers of fine textiles or garment assembly workers, Irish people in general have moved into more proactively creative roles in fashion—as designers and design educators, as magazine editors, organizers of catwalk shows and design competitions; as boutique buyers, bloggers, customizers, and keen consumers at every level of the market. The vibrancy of this fashion culture is not directly related to international commercial success: the recent recession-related struggles experienced by DFW, while local "lifestyle" events continue to grow and flourish amply illustrate this point. However, it is undoubtedly the case that established fashion trade events such as DFW, as well as Irish designers' international success—at London Fashion Week, for instance—underpin the fashion confidence of the popular media and that of the population more generally, albeit in a more subtle and long-term context.

Thus, it is clear that while Irish people engage on many levels with global fashion culture, they are also creating "fashion communities" at local level, where the excitement and creativity that is integral to fashion is celebrated, re-created, and communicated in an aesthetic discourse that is integrated in a meaningful way with other aspects of social and cultural life.

## Notes

1. Newspaper advertisements of the 1950s, for instance, would regularly highlight "nationally famous makers" and list Irish designers and brands of both clothing and fabric.
2. The following designer/clothing company websites were consulted in the preparation of this section of the article: www.johnrocha.ie; www.louisekennedy.com; www.laineykeogh.com; www.quinanddonnelly.ie; www.joannehynes.com; www.sphereone.biz; www.carolinemitchell.com; www.irishknitwearonline.com; www.inismeain.ie.
3. Signs have recently appeared in Penneys' stores advising customers to reassure themselves regarding the company's trading practices by consulting www.ethicalprimark.ie.
4. Examples in the Munster region would be Ela Maria, Bella Sola, and Kimono, all in Newcastle West, Co. Limerick; The County Boutique, Ennis, Co. Clare; Samui, Cork city; Tippe Canoe, Limerick city. Anecdotal evidence suggests that people travel in groups (sometimes from cities to the smaller towns) to the larger, more mainstream boutiques before a special occasion such as a wedding, while the promotion and advertising of the smaller ones stress the unusual and interesting labels stocked in them.

5. Various editions of the following magazines and their websites were consulted for this section of the article: *Image*, www.image.ie; *Irish Tatler*, www.harmonia.ie; *Prudence*, www.prudence.ie; *Limerick Now*, www.goldenegg.ie; *RSVP*, www.rsvp.ie; *VIP*, www.vipmagazine.ie.

## References


Ballard, Linda-May 2000. "Material Evidence: Dress as a Historical Record." In Trefor M. Owen (ed.) *From Corrib to Cultra: Folklife Essays in Honour of Alan Gailey*, pp. 62–70. Belfast: Institute of Irish Studies.

Clear, Caitriona. 2008. "The Minimum Rights of Every Woman?: women's changing appearance in Ireland, 1940–1966." *Irish Economic and Social History* XXXV: 68–80.

de Cléir, Síle. 2002. "Bhí bród as sin i gcónaí: cruthaitheacht agus cultúr na mban i dtraidisiún fheisteas Oileáin Árann." *Béascna, Journal of Folklore and Ethnology* 1: 85–99.

Dunlevy, Mairead. 1989. *Dress in Ireland: A History*. London: Batsford.

Egan, Barry. 2009. "Get Smart for an Absolutely Fabulous Fashion Event in Kerry." *Sunday Independent* March 22. http://www.independent.ie/entertainment/news-gossip (accessed April 28, 2010).

Epoch. 2009. *Epoch—Vintage, Recycled Fashion and Design Boutique, Dublin* [online]. http://www.fashion.ie (accessed October 8, 2010).

Etsy Ireland. 2010. *Belfast's Fashion Souk* [online] http://etsyireland.blogspot.com (accessed October 8, 2010).

Fallon, Brian. 1998. *An Age of Innocence: Irish Culture 1930–1960*. Dublin: Gill and Macmillan.

Harris, Constance. 2010. "Make Mine an Irish." *Sunday Independent—Life* magazine January 24: 24–9.

Haughton, Jonathan. 2008. "Historical Background." In John O'Hagan and Carol Newman (eds) *The Economy of Ireland: National and Sectoral Policy Issues*, pp. 2–28. Dublin: Gill and Macmillan.

Helland, Janice. 2007. *British and Irish Home Arts and Industries 1880–1914: Marketing Craft, Making Fashion*. Dublin: Irish Academic Press.

Intertrade Ireland. 2000. *Clothing and Footwear: An Ireland Retail Perspective*. Newry, Co. Down: Intertrade Ireland.

ICATA. 2005. "*Situation in the Irish Textile and Apparel Market 2005.*" Dublin: Irish Clothing and Textile Alliance.

ICATA. 2010. *Sector Profile* [online]. http://www.ibec.ie/Sectors/ICATA (accessed March 18, 2010).

Libra Designs. 2009. *Libra: Beautiful Clothes by Creative Designers* [online]. http://www.libradesigns.com/ (accessed April 28, 2010).

McClintock, H.F. 1950. *Old Irish and Highland Dress, and That of the Isle of Man*. Dundalk: Dundalgan Press.

McCrum, Elizabeth, 1996. *Fabric and Form: Irish fashion since 1950*, Belfast: Ulster Museum.

McQuillan, Deirdre. 2010a. "Pushing Boundaries." *Irish Times* magazine January 23: 16–17.

McQuillan, Deirdre. 2010b. "Rising Stars of Fashion." *Irish Times* magazine February 6: 14–16.

McQuillan, Deirdre. 2010c. "Turning the Inside Out." *Irish Times* magazine February 27: cover and pp. 10–11.

McQuillan, Deirdre. 2010d. "Something for Everyone." *Irish Times* magazine October 30: 26.

O'Brien, Peter. 2005. Interview on *Off the Rails* TV program, RTÉ 1, January 26: 8.30 pm.

O'Byrne, Robert, 2000a. *After a Fashion: A History of the Irish Fashion Industry*. Dublin: Town House.

O'Byrne, Robert. 2000b. "The Mink and Diamonds of Irish Fashion: Sybil Connolly." In *Irish Arts Review Yearbook 2000*, Vol. 16, pp. 109–119. Dublin: Irish Arts Review Ltd.

Ó Cléirigh, Nellie and Veronica Rowe. 1995. *Limerick Lace: A Social History and a Maker's Manual*. Gerrard's Cross: Colin Smythe.

Ó Crualaoich, Gearóid. 2003. *The Book of the Cailleach: Stories of the Wise-Woman Healer*. Cork: Cork University Press.

Ó Gráda, Cormac. 1999. *Black '47 and Beyond: The Great Irish Famine in History, Economy and Memory*. Princeton, NJ: Princeton University Press.

O'Kelly, Hilary. 1992. "Reconstructing Irishness: Dress in the Celtic Revival, 1880-1920." In Elizabeth Wilson and Juliet Ash (eds) *Chic Thrills: A Fashion Reader*, pp. 75–83. London: Pandora.

Rediscovery Centre. 2010. *About Rediscovery Centre* [online]. http://www.rediscoverycentre.ie (accessed October 8, 2010).

Regan, Lisa. 2008. "Move over London ... Introducing Galway Fashion Week." *Galway Independent* April 9. http://www.galwayindependent.com/local-news (accessed April 13, 2010).

Rowlands, Penelope. 2005. *A Dash of Daring: Carmel Snow and Her Life in Fashion, Art and Letters*. New York: Atria Books.

Scally, Derek. 2010. "The True Cost of Low Prices." *Irish Times* magazine January 16: 8–10.

Shaw-Smith, David. 1984. *Ireland's Traditional Crafts*. London: Thames & Hudson.

Steele, Valerie. 1988. *Paris Fashion: A Cultural History*. Oxford: Oxford University Press.

Taylor, Lou. 2002. *The Study of Dress History*. Manchester: Manchester University Press.

*Fashion Theory,* Volume 15, Issue 2, pp. 225–238
DOI: 10.2752/175174111X12954359478762
Reprints available directly from the Publishers.
Photocopying permitted by licence only.

# Portuguese Fashion Design Emerging Between Dictatorship and Fast Fashion

**Paula da Costa Soares**

Paula da Costa Soares has a PhD in Management and Design, Minho University; an MA in Marketing and Design, Minho University; and is Researcher at the CITAD—Centre for Research in Planning, Architecture and Design and lecturer at the School of Architecture and Arts, Lusíada University, Porto.
pcostasoares@gmail.com

## Abstract

Since the 1974 Revolution, all aspects of Portuguese society have gone through profound changes, and fashion and dress are no exception. Fashion design in Portugal took its first steps in the 1970s, conquering slowly yet progressively Portuguese consumers and, in more recent years, obtained a certain degree of international confidence and recognition. The Portuguese fashion industry has for many years been known for its quality and low-cost production, but designers face a larger challenge when it comes to being recognized as a fashion center. This article documents the period from 1974 to 2010 during which Portuguese fashion

**designers, events, and brands worked together to achieve national and international acknowledgment.**

**KEYWORDS: Portugal, fashion design, identity, fashion show, democracy**

After the so-called Carnation Revolution of April 25, 1974, which put an end to the right-wing dictatorship that had governed the country since 1926, Portugal embarked on a process of profound restructuring to find its place in Europe. This was a huge transformation of all aspect of society, including fashion design. At this time, Portuguese fashion began to take its first steps, initially with some fashion events and a very small number of local designers' ateliers, and later, with the opening of fashion schools and the National Costume Museum.

Historically, Portuguese designer fashion has emerged between two "bookends," which in different ways have limited the potential of the designer fashion sector. The first bookend is the dictatorship, which lasted until the 1974 Revolution. It was only in the post-revolutionary period that the Portuguese began to have free access to fashion from abroad and national fashion design, that is original designs from Portuguese designers, as opposed to copies of international styles, began to appear. The other bookend is the commercial development of clothing markets, most notably the Zara fast fashion format, which since the 1980s has had a massive influence on Portuguese style and is largely responsible for the changes in Portuguese fashion brand offerings. In the early period, development of independent and distinctive fashion design was restricted by the lack of democracy and civil freedom. In the latter period, the extreme market conditions of fast fashion undermine the business opportunities for Portuguese fashion designers. Locked between these two restricting factors, the development of Portuguese fashion design has never had the ambition of turning Lisbon or Porto into genuine fashion centers, but simply that Portuguese designer labels should be recognized at home and abroad.

## Portuguese Fashion before 1974

Forty-eight years (1926–74) of dictatorship, censorship, and political persecution isolated Portugal from the world. As a consequence of the domestic political situation access to international fashion or fashion information functioned as a sign of social distinction, and ensured a trickle-down adoption of fashion, reflecting enormous social and economic differences (Barreiro 1998; Sproles 1981). Parisian *haute couture* and its couturiers, as well as the terms "*haute couture*" and "ready-to-wear," were unfamiliar to practically everyone, but the highest social classes had access to French fashion through the couture ateliers in Lisbon (Teixeira 2000).

These ateliers began to appear in the late 1920s and French fashion was redesigned for ladies in dressmakers' ateliers, who carefully adapted the Parisian *haute couture* designs, using French fabrics, to the individual taste and bodies of their clients. The first of these couture ateliers, coming to have the most important influence on Portuguese fashion and dress in the 1930s and 1940s, belonged to Madame do Vale, established in Lisbon (Teixeira 2000). Later, it was Ana Maravilhas who best represented Portuguese *haute couture*, traveling to Paris to buy designer items and fabrics from couturiers such as Dior, Balmain, and Balenciaga, and adapting them to Portuguese taste and needs. The design process was similar to the one followed by Madame do Vale—copy and redesign to client needs and taste—but Ana Maravilhas also presented each collection at her atelier in small fashion shows (Soares 2010a; Coelho and Avillez 1987).

Another influence on Portuguese fashion and style came from the European refugees who came to Portugal before and during World War II. Unlike the couture ateliers the refugees were in contact with all social classes, bringing with them not only clothing and jewelry from different cultures but also knowledge about styles and dressmaking. Some women refugees created and presented their own clothing and hat collections; for example, Rosy Pollack, a Jewish refugee from Poland, presented knitwear and jersey collections that were highly appreciated among the Portuguese upper classes and foreign royalty in exile (Teixeira 2000).

The desire for fashionable clothing among the lower social classes was fulfilled by domestic production or through dressmakers who copied fashion design items from magazines or from the ateliers' collections, using inexpensive fabric but with a similar texture and color to the original. It was also quite common to reuse parents' clothing for children and garments belonging to older children were remade for younger children, in a continuous recycling of fabrics necessitated by the low incomes of many families (Soares 2010a).

The authoritarian regime became more repressive during the 1950s, and in the 1960s, as in the rest of Europe, fashion became a way to communicate and protest. By the mid-1960s, stores such as Loja das Meias and Porfírios began to import clothes for young people and to spread London fashion to the main Portuguese cities, changing their dress style (Soares 2010a; Teixeira 2000; Coelho and Avillez 1987). Loja das Meias was the first store to trade international brands, like Levi's, but the store that most influenced young Portuguese style was Porfírios, which offered fashion items copied from London fashion manufactured in Portugal with Portuguese materials (Coelho and Avillez 1987). The difference between generations and lifestyle was, by the end of the 1960s, becoming obvious on the streets of the main Portuguese cities—it was an early sign of the profound transformations that were about to come to Portuguese society.

Even so, the Portuguese people still had little hope for their future, in particular because many young men were sent to fight in the wars of the right-wing government. The horrors of the Overseas Colonial War, fought against the independence movements in Angola, Mozambique, and Guinea-Bissau, as well as the necessary decolonization of the African colonies increased people's distrust in the political regime and despair in the future (Mattoso 1995a). The economic and social situation, fraught with political persecution, was aggravated at the beginning of the 1970s, as protest movements increased. However, freedom was given back to the Portuguese by the Movement of Armed Forces (MFA), through a revolution with no violent conflicts and fully supported by the Portuguese people in 1974 (Rodrigues 1997; Mattoso 1995b).

## After the 1974 Revolution

The years that followed the Carnation Revolution were intense in the struggle for economic stability, democracy, and human rights. Artists exiled abroad returned home and art exhibitions proliferated, books were published on most varied themes, films were produced, and new buildings were designed. "Freedom and democracy were the order of the day," also in terms of dress (Teixeira 2000: 189). Newly won rights for women led not only to an adjustment in family structures, but also to a sexual revolution (Mattoso 1995b). This was reflected in the Portuguese dress style. The hippie look was taken on by almost everyone and signs of wealth were banished from the streets and considered fascist—Portuguese people could finally express themselves freely, and dress was the main code of a new way of life and thinking, even if this new style was imported from other countries (Duarte 2005; Teixeira 2000).

In this climate of democracy and freedom, Portuguese fashion designers started to learn the business of fashion by copying and redesigning dress and items from foreign fashion designers. In this respect, designers such as Ana Salazar, Manuela Gonçalves, and Manuela Tojal can be considered the first generation of Portuguese fashion designers, as opposed to the dressmakers of an earlier period. Each has a distinctive approach and background, reflecting the fact that there was no formal education in fashion design, and therefore no standard for a fashion designer's career trajectory.

Influenced by London fashion, Ana Salazar opened her first store in 1972 in Lisbon. Initially she presented redesigned imported clothes and accessories, although with a very personal signature and unusual details (Coelho and Avillez 1987). Based on the knowledge acquired in this type of business, Ana Salazar started up her own brand of denim clothing—-*Harlow*—available at her stores but also directed at export (Coelho and Avillez 1987). In 1984, Ana Salazar launched her own label, devoted to a sensual, strong-minded woman, aware of her femininity, a reflection of the new woman that emerged from the Revolution. Her design was irreverent, characterized by pure geometry in which diagonal cuts and usual details predominated, and also by the use of dark colors, especially black. She was, additionally, the first Portuguese fashion designer to go abroad to show her collections in 1988 and became known as "*La Portugaise*" in Paris by the fashion press (Guedes and Soares 2005; Teixeira 2000; Figure 1).

By contrast, Manuela Gonçalves was one of the first designers with formal training in fashion design abroad in London. The strong influences from Japanese fashion design are obvious in her conceptual and artistic approach to clothing and as the designer states: "I don't like to be known

**Figure 1**
Ana Salazar, Fall/Winter 2010 Collection. Image courtesy of Portugal Fashion Organization.

for doing fashion, I prefer to be known for creating clothes" (Coelho and Avillez 1987: 88). One of her main design characteristics is that shape is built from raw and natural materials and the human body stands as the structure, possible because all the production processes involve manual sewing methods. Another feature, also very characteristic of her designs, are the multiple functions that an item can have when used.

Manuela Tojal began to work as a designer in the late 1970s. At the beginning of her career, she was involved in the teaching of fashion and, in the late 1980s, in the coordination of the PORTEX shows, a specialized fair where collections from the main national exporters were first shown. However, her recognition as a fashion designer occurred with the opening of her first shop. During the 1990s, her collections were increasingly handmade, resembling fairytales, in which the woman is revealed both as feminine and docile, in the role of a fairy, and, at the same time, as rebellious and urban, in the role of *femme fatale*. Manuela Tojal's fashion process, with no heed to fashion trends, was to design each item from the material, in a continuous handmade process, where fabric painting and details were important to tell the fashion story of each item (Soares 1999).

By the end of the 1970s and during the 1980s, the couture ateliers that had been so important during the dictatorship gradually closed down, and numerous local ready-to-wear stores started to appear in the main cities of Portugal. However, one of the main influences at this time on the Portuguese way of life and dress came from the other side of the Atlantic, from Brazilian and American soap operas, such *Gabriela*, *Dallas*, and *Dynasty*, and the Yuppie style was adopted. Instead of France, the main foreign influence on Portuguese fashion now came from Pan-American media culture.

## Organizing Portuguese Fashion

In the years from the end of the 1970s to the beginning of the 1990s, a number of organizations were built that institutionalized Portuguese fashion, and ensured a market and an audience for domestic creative design. These include the National Costume Museum in Lisbon, fashion shows and similar events that started to take place, and fashion schools and national fashion associations that appeared in response to market needs.

The decision to create a National Costume Museum came from the huge success of the Civil Costume Exhibition at the National Museum of Ancient Art, in 1974, which led to the donation of many costumes and accessories from private collections (www.museudotraje-ipmuseus.pt). Since it opened in 1977 the museum has played a major role not only in exhibiting historical clothing and accessories, but also in promoting new national and international talent in clothing accessories and jewelry design through thematic exhibitions and its catalogs. Ever since the mid-1980s, accessories and textile design by contemporary artists and fashion designers also play a major role in the museum's exhibitions. Today, the museum's main goal is the collection of art, fashion and dress documents, folklore costumes, fabrics and textiles, and apparel manufacturing tools, but toys with historical and ethnographic interest are also collected (Cabral 2005).

Lisbon in the late 1970s was also the scene for a series of fashion events, which, using Valerie Steele's terms, can be seen as "ritualized fashion display" (de Cléir 2010; Steele 1988: 285). Ana Salazar held the *Acontecimentos de Moda* (which translates as *Fashion Happenings*), a dynamic show where the catwalk allowed a reading of all fashion proposals and, at the same time, included performances in which the audience participated actively. Thus, Ana Salazar is also responsible for encouraging fashion in Portugal through free-access fashion shows and other events produced for the general public. In 1986, another fashion event took place—the *Manobras de Maio* (*May Manoeuvres*, indicating an underground happening) show was held alternately in the historic boulevards of Lisbon and Porto. This fashion show presented a mystical environment especially devised for each collection, intended to help new designers become better known and raise awareness in the Portuguese market (Soares 2010b; Teixeira 2000).

At the same time, trade associations such as ANIVEC/APIV—Portuguese Textile and Clothing Association—supported education in fashion and textile design. This association is linked to the CITEX school in Porto founded in 1981 (www.citex.pt), an undergraduate training institute, offering courses in fashion and textiles, to prepare young designers for work in the industry (Coelho and Avillez 1987). In addition, other fashion schools established in the 1980s were CITEM in Lisbon, analogous to CITEX in aiming to educate professionals for the fashion industry, and GUDI in Porto, which focused on couture as opposed to fashion design, and which has lost its reputation in recent years. However, Portuguese industry was not ready to receive this new generation of well-educated personnel, but continued to opt for a market-driven approach of redesigning models from other European fashion centers (Soares 2007). This incomplete and less expensive process of design, along with the identification of Portugal as a production country, is one of the main reasons why Portuguese fashion has found it difficult to be recognized in a national and international context.

ANIVEC/APIV was also responsible for PORTEX, a biannual specialized trade fair where collections from the main national exporters were first shown and where Manuela Tojal was part of the fashion shows' organization (Soares 1999). Currently, PORTEX no longer exists and FILMODA is now the only fashion trade fair in Portugal, taking place twice a year, in Lisbon. Since the 1990s, ModaLisboa and

Portugal Fashion are the main catwalk events and the major promoters of Portuguese fashion design domestically and abroad. But they pursue different goals. ModaLisboa, initially an event to promote designers and their ready-to-wear creations within and beyond Portuguese borders, is currently one of the most widely recognized fashion events in Portugal. Eduarda Abondanza and Matos Ribeiro, two fashion designers that worked with Ana Salazar at the beginning of their career (Coelho and Avillez 1987), are responsible for these fashion events, that have become the "main fashion venue for Portuguese fashion" (Teixeira 2000: 233). ModaLisboa shows are divided into three catwalks, catering to an emerging new community with a special taste for fashion: industrial design, new talents, and new designers (Soares 2010b).

At a time when the Portuguese clothing industry was popular for its cheap yet quality production, rather than for its design, ANJE—National Association of Young Entrepreneurs—and ANIVEC organized Portugal Fashion, a biannual event that aimed to promote fashion design nationally and internationally (Oliveira 2005). It is based on the idea that competitive prices do not remain unchanged, that the industry itself demanded the integration of production with design by establishing partnerships between designers and the fashion industry, and that there was a huge need to promote Portuguese fashion abroad (Oliveira 2005). Fashion shows in New York, Paris, São Paulo, and Barcelona have thus been organized and broadcast on Fashion TV, and the support to young designers at international events, such as Elizabeth Teixeira's participation at the IAF International Designer Award—India (www.portugalfashion.com), can be seen as a good example of the efforts made to internationalize fashion made in Portugal.

In the years preceding the new millennium, fashion designed in Portugal took the first steps towards strengthening its position nationally and the media began to promote the work of Portuguese designers. Portuguese versions of fashion magazines, such as *Maxima*, *Elle*, *Marie Claire*, and the Portuguese *Moda&Moda*, were the media vehicles used to spread Portuguese fashion (Teixeira 2000), and some of the Portuguese designers gained recognition in the national market through these publications.

## Fashion Designers from the 1990s until Now

Every year promising new designers are introduced to the Portuguese fashion scene, but only a few present new collections in catwalk shows, create their own label or open their own atelier or store. The majority of the recognized Portuguese designers in Portugal began to show their collections at ModaLisboa or Portugal Fashion, most of them studied fashion design at CITEX, and have an atelier or store in Porto. And, even though they follow different fashion styles and approaches or related influences, these fashion designers have an implicit concern with product design and manufacturing and a belief in the value of Portuguese fashion design—an idea that is learned at fashion schools but is also a reflection of the concern with the national and international recognition of "Portuguese Fashion."

The Portuguese fashion designers presented here are those who have obtained greater recognition in the Portuguese market in the last fifteen years and are still working and presenting collections at their stores and on Portuguese catwalks. Although they do not share a similar style, it is possible to relate influences or fashion image in their work. José António Tenente and Luís Buchinho are good examples of designers who gradually gain recognition through the Portuguese fashion media and in the national market through their participation at fashion events like ModaLisboa and Portugal Fashion. Their fashion style is best described as a combination of the classic with current influences in an exceptionally minimalist and sober product. Tenente's design is defined by strong influences from the fine arts, in the handling of volume, in a taste for perfection, and in the creative austerity applied to the organization of his collections. Luís Buchinho's collections, also with strong influences from the arts and comic books, blend femininity with comfort and elegance for the urban woman, usually in a dark color palette. Since 1998, Buchinho has participated in Paris Fashion Week, as well as in the sixth and seventh New York Fashion Weeks, from 2000 on (Figure 2).

The most internationally recognized Portuguese fashion designers are Fátima Lopes and Felipe Oliveira Baptista. Fátima Lopes' collections are renowned for their extraordinarily exuberant and feminine sensuality in her own unique style, with some aggressive features. She has, like Luís Buchinho, been a regular participant at Paris Fashion Week since 1999. In 1998, she presented a bikini in gold and diamonds in Paris, which became known as the most expensive bikini in the world, leading to many invitations for the establishment of partnerships with jewelry brands. Felipe Oliveira Baptista studied fashion design at Kingston University, worked for MaxMara, Christophe Lemaire, and Cerruti, and currently designs for Lacoste and for his own label in Paris. He has received a number of fashion awards such as the Grand Prix at the Festival D'Hières and the ANDAM/LVMH Fashion Award.

One of the most widely recognized fashion designers in the Portuguese market is Miguel Vieira. His label can be found on several fashion products, mainly clothing and footwear, having become established in the fashion industry with women's and men's clothing during the late 1980s. The label is commercialized in multi-brand stores, a distribution strategy that has made him the most renowned fashion designer with the highest sales revenue in the Portuguese market. His career path is atypical in the Portuguese designers fashion context; Miguel Vieira started to work as a fashion brand for the national market and only

**Figure 2**
Luís Buchinho, Fall/Winter 2010 collection. Image courtesy of Portugal Fashion Organization.

later began to participate as a fashion designer in the most diverse fashion events in Portugal.

Anabela Baldaque launched a women's clothing brand in the late 1980s but it was only in the 1990s that she pursued an internationalization strategy by participating in a number of fashion events through Portugal Fashion (Paris, Barcelona, and, more recently, in São Paulo). Her collections reflect her way of life, with simplicity and romanticism she creates sensual but discrete and feminine stories (Figure 3).

Another Portuguese designer, appearing on the Portuguese fashion scene at the turn of the millennium, who also works the feminine

**Figure 3**
Anabela Baldaque, Fall/Winter 2010 collection. Image courtesy of Portugal Fashion Organization.

romantic look, is Katty Xiomara. Her creations, with simple silhouettes and shaped in a rich mixture of patterns, colors, and textures, are known to be elegant and poetic.

Nuno Gama and Maria Gambina design clothing with a clearly visible popular culture influence. Nuno Gama is the Portuguese designer who most extols Portuguese culture in his collections, because of his search for inspiration in Portuguese textile heritage and culture. Maria Gambina won the New Designers competition twice at ModaLisboa in the early 1990s. She has a unique style that has achieved broad acceptance in the Portuguese context: practical, colorful, multifunctional clothing, inspired by the streets and music. Some of the themes that have already been a source of inspiration for her are not related to fashion trends, but rather to people, based on Brazilian music, disco-funk, and jazz or on more exotic countries, such as Jamaica or Thailand.

Anabela Baldaque, Nuno Gama, Maria Gambina, and Katty Xiomara began to work as designers, with their own labels, during the 1990s. Even with different fashion approaches and fashion education at CITEX, they are examples of the third generation of Portuguese designers that began their professional careers in a social context where Portuguese fashion was already accepted by the national market and where fashion events were already a constant in the main cities of Portugal.

## Fast Fashion

In the last few years in Portugal, the evolution of the consumer and producer market predicts a constant need for innovation, at an increasingly more intense pace, in shorter time frames, due to the rapid expansion these markets are undergoing. At the same time, the Portuguese fashion industry and fashion designers face progressive globalization and foreign competition, which result in benefits to the Portuguese consumer, huge fashion choices at low prices.

In the last thirty years, there has been a strong discrepancy between the Portuguese designer fashion sector, described above, and the clothing industry as a whole. The Portuguese clothing industry has always been dedicated to production, not to design, and Portugal was, and still is known for its high-quality production. The collections of some Portuguese brands were created, or redesigned, from collections of other European brands with the same fashion image (Agis *et al.* 2001; Soares 1999), and a great part of the Portuguese clothing industry survives by manufacturing for international brands or companies (Soares 2007). There are only a small number of clothing manufacturers with their own label, a complete design process, and marketing plan.

In 1986, Zara opened its first store in Porto, the first one outside Spanish borders, and soon began to influence the consumer and the clothing habits of Portuguese society. Despite some initial misgivings, Zara quickly imposed its fashion concept, due not only to low prices when compared to Portuguese brands, but also to its fast renewal of stocks, which satisfied the new predisposition to consume of Portuguese people, and to its store-based marketing and simplified sales strategy (Soares 1999, 2007). Nowadays, the Inditex brands still correspond to Portuguese consumer fashion needs, with different fashion formats and their presence in all the shopping centers in Portugal, and it still is the main influence on Portuguese dress.

The response from Portuguese brand companies to this new commercial trend took some time to surface and, despite an evident increase in market share, they could not match the Zara phenomenon. Salsa, Throttleman, and Lanidor are some of the Portuguese brands that have gradually gained the Portuguese consumers' trust since the beginning of the 1990s. Even working for different market groups and with diverse fashion styles, they are the most renowned Portuguese brands in the national market, due to their product design and integrated marketing communication—especially in terms of visual merchandising or communication at the point-of-sale. The trade of these brands in mono-brand stores in shopping centers, along with the quality offered in both design and products has, in spite of their medium–high price range, increased their recognition as fashion brands in the national market.

## Conclusion

Portuguese fashion design emerged between two bookends: the dictatorship that lasted until the 1974 Revolution and the appearance of fast fashion in the Portuguese market during the 1980s. Before the 1974 Revolution, fashion in Portugal was a redesign of French fashion made by Portuguese couturiers and later had influences from abroad, such as the influences from the European refugees of World War II. After the 1974 Revolution, when the first Portuguese fashion designers had already began to show their work in the national market, the main influence in Portuguese dress was once again from abroad, from Pan-American media culture and London designer fashion.

The second bookend, the appearance of Zara in the late 1980s, and other fast fashion brands during the 1990s, completely changed the behavior of the Portuguese fashion consumer, and the offer of new fashion concepts and marketing approaches was the response from Portuguese brands to this new market competitor. Nowadays, all the Inditex formats still have great influence on Portuguese dress style and represent the biggest problem Portuguese industries have to face in the Portuguese fashion market.

Portuguese fashion designers, despite all the efforts through their stores and catwalk shows, are still a long way from international recognition. Even in Portugal they are known mostly because of a certain amount of media coverage, although not necessarily from the fashion media, and their participation in ModaLisboa and Portugal Fashion throughout the years. In the face of such a competitive reality, it becomes imperative for Portuguese companies to develop renewed efforts, particularly those that have been less open to new concepts and to new areas in the process of the development and management of fashion collections, as a way to build a strong and well-established image. However, Portugal still has to struggle for a place in the fashion world. The goal is not to be accepted as a new fashion center, but merely to obtain recognition of Portuguese fashion within and beyond borders.

## References


Agis, D., J. Gouveia and P. Vaz. 2001. *Vestindo o futuro: macrotendências para as indústrias têxtil, vestuário e moda até 2020*. Porto: APIM.

Barreiro, A.M. 1998. *Mirar Y Hacerse Mirar: La moda en las sociedades modernas*. Madrid: Tecnos.

Cabral, L.M. 2005. *As histórias que as roupas contam*. http://dn.sapo.pt/inicio/interior.aspx?content_id=616137 (accessed March 30, 2007).

Cleir, S. de. 2010. "Ireland." In J.B. Eicher and L. Skov (eds) *Berg Encyclopedia of World Dress and Fashion Western Europe*, Vol. 8, *West Europe*, pp. 314–19. Oxford: Berg.

Coelho, T. and M.A. Avillez. 1987. *A Moda em Portugal nos Últimos Trinta Anos*. Lisbon: Edições Rolim.

Duarte, C.L. 2005. *Moda Portuguesa*. Porto: CTT Correios de Portugal.

Guedes, G. and P.C. Soares. 2005. "Branding of Fashion Products: A Communication Process, a Marketing Approach." In *Proceedings of the ABC 7th European Convention, Business Communication: Making an Impact*, Copenhagen. http://www.businesscommunication.org/conventionsNew/proceedingsNew/2005New/PDFs/25ABCEurope05.pdf (accessed December 31, 2010).

Mattoso, J. 1995a. *História de Portugal—O Estado Novo (1926–1985)*. Lisbon: Editorial Estampa.

Mattoso, J. 1995b. *História de Portugal—Portugal em Transe (1974–1985)*. Lisbon: Editorial Estampa.

Oliveira, G. 2005. "Portugal Fashion: 10 anos a mudar a moda em Portugal." *Jornal de Notícias* October 28: 20–2.

Rodrigues, A.A. 1997. *História comparada—Portugal, Europa e o Mundo*, Vol. 2. Lisbon: Temas e Debates Editora.

Soares, P. C. 1999. "Desenvolvimento e Gestão de Colecções de Vestuário." Unpublished MA thesis in Design and Marketing, Minho University, Guimarães, Portugal.

Soares, P.C. 2007. "Comunicação Integrada de Colecções de Produtos de Moda." unpublished PhD thesis in Design and Management, Minho University, Guimarães, Portugal.

Soares, P.C. 2010a. "Portugal." In J.B. Eicher and L. Skov (eds) *Encyclopedia of World Dress and Fashion*, Vol. 8, *West Europe*, pp. 279–82. Oxford: Berg.

Soares, P.C. 2010b. "Snapshot: Fashion Events in Portugal." In J.B. Eicher and L. Skov (eds) *Encyclopedia of World Dress and Fashion*, Vol. 8, *West Europe*, pp. 282–83. Oxford: Berg.

Sproles, G.B. 1981. "Analyzing Fashion Life Cycles—Principles and Perspectives." *Journal of Marketing* 45: 116–24.

Steele, V. 1988. *Paris Fashion: A Cultural History*. Oxford: Oxford University.

Teixeira, M.B. 2000. *A Moda do Século 1900–2000*. Lisbon: Museu Nacional do Traje.

*Fashion Theory,* Volume 15, Issue 2, pp. 239–258
DOI: 10.2752/175174111X12954359478807
Reprints available directly from the Publishers.
Photocopying permitted by licence only.

# The New Nordic Cool: Björk, Icelandic Fashion, and Art Today

**Æsa Sigurjónsdóttir**

Æsa Sigurjónsdóttir D.E.A. is assistant professor at the Faculty of Icelandic and Comparative Cultural Studies, University Iceland. She is Dr Kristján Eldjárn Research Fellow at National Museum Iceland. Recent publications include contributions to *Berg Encyclopedia of World Dress and Fashion* (2010), *Icelandic Art Today* (2009), and her book *Fashion and Identity in Dress and Photography: Iceland 1860–1960* (National Museum Iceland, 2008).
aesas@hi.is

## Abstract

It was only in the early twenty-first century that Icelandic fashion captured international attention, and Icelandic designers started dreaming of recognition in the global fashion system. Over the last decade, they have oscillated between affirming a cosmopolitan vision of the trendy North, and a commercial desire to brand their products with an identity rooted in the image of nature. Inspired by the international success of Björk as a global style icon, the young Icelandic fashion designers now dream of stepping forward as an "avant-garde" in the international fashion world.

**KEYWORDS: Iceland, fashion design, identity, place, nature**

In her book *The National Fabric: Fashion, Britishness, Globalization* (2005), Alison L. Goodrum, argues "that the apparently straightforward and economically driven process to do with globalization of fashion is, in fact, a far more culturally nuanced and locally embedded encounter than has previously been suggested" (2005: 12). Local embeddedness well describes the situation in Iceland as analyzed by New-York-based art critic Gregory Volk, who wrote that young Icelandic artists have their homeland always at the back of their mind.

> One thing you do notice [...] is that no matter how internationally minded Icelandic artists are (and almost all have studied and lived abroad), eventually the country itself comes to figure in their work: as a physical locus, as a trove of images and materials or—more mysteriously for outsiders—as a comprehensive force with which one is perpetually in dialogue. It's not that the compelling work now being produced is about Iceland in any literal sense. Far from it. But Iceland is nevertheless there, in the deep grain of the inquiry, a constant presence that can be approached with a sense of wonder, humor or irony, via poetic engagement or tough-minded criticism. (Volk 2000)

Perhaps this obsession with a place is a characteristic of small nations? At least Volk's sharp-eyed analysis of the Icelandic art scene in year 2000 is still relevant and can be adapted to fashion and design today. Like Icelandic artists, fashion designers have been more self-conscious than business-minded, reflecting a deep concern with identity construction and search for difference.

In this article I explore how the desire for structure and identity is embodied in contemporary art, fashion, and culture. I suggest that the narratives and visual constructions produced by fashion designers are the result of many factors, both historical and economic. They can be identified as being representations of postcolonial hybridity, in which artists and designers translate information from one format to another (Bourriaud 2009), or simply react against standardization and commercialism in global contexts.

In *Hybridity and its Discontents*, Avtar Brah and Annie Coombes describe hybridity as a "key concept in cultural criticism, in post-colonial studies, in debates about cultural contestation and appropriation, and in relation to the concept of the border and the ideal of cosmopolitanism" (2000: 1). The word hybridity is used to describe the contemporary creolization of cultures and of technologies, considered not as "pure," but mixed, often symptomatic of a postcolonial situation. In the case of Iceland, the hybridity in question is not rooted in cultural diversity, or in tension or contestation with the colonizer, but in its position on the border of Europe, a community in search for cultural singularity and difference, which is based on geographical and historical ideas of otherness.

Equally characteristic is the systematic crossover between art, fashion, music, and the extensive use of new media. For this reason, the use of the definition of hybridization made by Nestor Garcia Canclini seems to be the most appropriate: "The word *hybridization* seems more ductile for the purpose of naming not only the mixing of ethnic or religious elements but the products of advanced technologies and modern or postmodern social processes" (2005: xxxiv).

The intensity that has characterized creativity in Iceland over the last decade is often associated with Iceland's postcolonial condition, represented in the constant need for reevaluation of identity. Iceland had to be refigured politically and economically after the end of the Cold War, and the economic meltdown in 2008 made reevaluation of cultural values still more urgent.

Björk's role has been essential. More than anyone else, she has influenced visual culture and contributed to the growth of the creative grassroot space that sparked the attention of international media in the early twenty-first century. Simultaneous to her ascent as a global fashion icon, she has collaborated with the most ambitious artists and film directors, retaining control of her own productions and actively commissioning various dresses and stage costumes. She has constantly referred to her Icelandic roots as an important source and inspiration for her creative process, indicating her "over-romantic ideal of uniting with nature" (Kennedy 2006). Her extravagant outfits function to translate difference, even weirdness, that she herself defines as signifying aspects of her "Icelandicness."

## Constructing Icelandic Identity in Dress and Fashion

Icelandic fashion is a relatively recent invention. The artist Sigurður Guðmundsson (1833–74) might be considered as the first Icelandic designer. After studying drawing and painting at the Royal Academy of Arts in Copenhagen he launched the idea of a specific national dress worn daily, and wrote the first account of Icelandic dress history published in 1857 (Guðmundsson 1857). His designs, which were based on research into traditional clothing, were also inspired by literature, botany, and ancient textiles, and lead to a national dress reform that took off in the year 1860 (Sigurjónsdóttir 2008). His motivation was European ideas about the cultural definition of nations as these were discussed by Scandinavian intellectuals of the period (Hálfdanarson 2001).

The national dress reform was not an organized movement concerned with renouncing modern fashion as such. Iceland was under the governance of Norwegian and Danish kings during the period 1262–1944. The country was part of the Crown of Denmark, and was regarded as one of the Danish provinces, rather than a colony (Ellenberger 2009). Guðmundsson's sartorial recommendations were at first similarly aimed against the Danish elites who dressed in contemporary French-style fashion. He insisted on the importance of defining and visualizing an individual public self, making use of dress as the quintessence of modern expression, and his version of national dress was conceived for urban space rather than for daily life in rural conditions. Icelandic women had to make choices, and the act of wearing the national dress was a personal statement, an important element in the process of nation building, a clear instance of Hobsbawm's "invention of tradition": " ... taken to mean a set of practices ... of a ritual or symbolic nature, which seek to inculcate certain values and norms of behavior by repetition, which automatically implies continuity with the past" (Hobsbawm and Ranger 1983: 1; Figure 1).

**Figure 1**
The national dress ("Peysuföt") was adapted to the taste of the moment and used as "Sunday best" during the first half of the twentieth century. Photograph: Anonymous studio photograph, 1916. Image courtesy Minjasafnid á Akureyri/ Hallgrímur Einarsson.

The national dresses appealed to women of all social categories, and the new designs proposed by Guðmundsson became a long-term success, a visual paradigm, an idea rather than a directive, that fed into the nationalist political process from 1860 to 1960. His ideas were reflected locally in dress revivals and updated national styles were created and adopted at critical historic moments, such as in 1874, when Iceland was granted a constitution by the King Christian IX, during the period of Home Rule (1904–18), during the visit of King Frederik VIII, the King of Denmark and Iceland, in 1907, at the Millenary Celebration of the Parliament in 1930, and finally in 1944 when Iceland finally became an independent state. Since then, the national dress has lost its everyday attraction, but has kept its place as attire for memorial occasions and as a formal dress of state (Sigurjónsdóttir 2008).

## Woolen Dreams

The creation of national industry marked the first half of the twentieth century. Nationalism became embedded in daily life, as in the consumption of everyday goods. Wool had a direct natural link to nature and the wool industry was considered to represent a modern industrial potential that would provide employment for the emerging working class. During the 1920s and 1930s, the wool industry grew rapidly and was appropriated to the notion of "patriotic" consumption, which became closely associated with wool products. Long woolen underpants were ironically named *föðurlandið* (the fatherland) and wearing "plus-fours" made from Icelandic tweed became a declaration of modernity, as if wool was a magical link between the past and the present (Sigurjónsdóttir 2008).

Production steadily shifted from the domestic sphere and small local factories were created for the production of outdoor and daily wear, for seamen and others working outside in the growing fishing industry. Traditional homemade outfits from sheep's wool and sheepskins were replaced by denim garments and oiled waterproofs (Sigurjónsdóttir 2008). Even though this history of industrial production is quite short, it became one of the authenticity elements conscripted in the successful branding campaign of Design Group Italia, Milan, orchestrated for the active wear 66°North and exemplified in their slogan: "Keeping Iceland warm since 1926" (Ingólfsson 2008).

Parallel to industrialization, domestic production continued. Knitting had been practiced by men and women since the sixteenth century, and wool, as I have indicated, retained its strong national connotations, as Icelandic sheep are the only remaining breed to naturally produce wool in several colors. The handcraft revivals led by women's associations that occurred in the late 1920s inspired creative experiments with wool both as material substance and as a final product, such as the sweaters, based on Norwegian and Swedish patterns. The most popular, the Lopi sweater, with its characteristic circular yoke and patterned borders, was created in the late 1950s and has retained its place as utilitarian garment, a tourist souvenir, as well as a fashion item (Sigurjónsdóttir 2008).

During the 1930s, fashion became an important element in the transformation of Reykjavik's urban space. Public places such as cinemas, restaurants, and dancehalls, became scenes for a small but fashionable crowd who sought to keep up with the latest international trends and display their own interpretations of fashionable styles. Scandinavian and American fashion and pattern magazines, such as *Nordisk Mønster-Tidende*, *Femina*, and *Fashion News*, were valuable for the local seamstresses. Fashion shows became a chic form of entertainment, starting in the mid-1930s, showing clothing made and designed in Iceland by tailors and dressmakers trained in Copenhagen or Berlin, many of whom ran successful local businesses (Sigurjónsdóttir 2008).

The 1930s witnessed a shift in cultural discourse and a corresponding redefinition of national identity. The modernist culture of the 1930s promoted a functionalist aesthetics, associated with new technologies and machinery. Photographic representations of nature and the vogue for wilderness hiking provided an alternative notion of the sublimity of nature. Both approaches replaced the historical references that figured in earlier periods. Modern agriculture and the industrialization of the fishing industry provided different models for a new conception of "Icelandicness." These were variously represented in the media of photography and film at the New York World Fair in 1939 (Ellenberger 2008).

Because of its geographical location, between Europe and America, Iceland became a strategic location during the Cold War period following the Second World War. American popular culture was a powerful influence on the1950s cultural scene through the US military base located in Keflavik. But the Soviet Union was also a close neighbor and woolen goods were exported both to the USA and the Soviet Union; thus Icelandic designs had to appeal to both US and Soviet markets (Guðmundsson 1988). This production became obsolete in the early 1990s and most factories were closed down and dismantled.

The Cold War was a framing condition not only for the wool industry, but also the emerging local fashion production during following decades. The first designer to have introduced urban male street fashion was the British tailor and designer Colin Porter (b. 1934). He arrived in Iceland in the mid-1950s as a representative of a British clothing company supplying civil clothing to the US army base. Soon he started designing menswear for local Icelandic companies, basing his style on British tailoring traditions, but later drew upon London street fashion (Sigurjónsdóttir 2008). Don Cano was another popular street wear brand created by the Swedish designer Jan Davidsson in 1979 and exported throughout the 1980s (Sigurðsson 2009). Foreign designers thus dominated production, as there were no Icelandic fashion designers practicing at the time. The market was small, as free import–export was restricted until Iceland became a member of the European Free Trade Association (EFTA) in 1970. However, it was only after the elimination of tariffs on industrial goods in trade between the EEC and the EFTA states in 1977 that free trade really took off (EFTA 2009).

## Björk

Björk (b. 1965) is indisputably one of the most innovative international style icons of recent decades. She is the ultimate global hybrid, making use of new media as the vehicle within which her persona is both projected and received. Famous for collaborating with iconoclasts, including designers such as Alexander McQueen, Marjan Pejoski, and Jeremy Scott, adored by international fashion and music media, she has influenced not only fashion on an international level, but visual popular culture in general.

Björk's style has its roots in Reykjavik post-punk culture, as documented in Friðrik Þór Friðriksson's film *Rokk í Reykjavík* (1982). Her style is grounded in the new kind of awareness, implicit social critique, and self-display, which started emerging in the 1980s among the younger generation, reacting against the national emblems and institutions that had been key elements in the nation-building process of the twentieth century.

Björk already figured as a fashion icon on the cover of the album released with the film-music track of *Rokk í Reykjavík*, wearing a frilly fairytale dress, her cheeks painted clownish red. Her masquerade look, a mix of Pierrot and Columbine, was in place. The film was a pioneering attempt to present Reykjavik as a city where avant-garde musical culture was thriving. It showcased a place-specific alternative scene, and thus helped to launch the idea that a nation considered as peripheral could nonetheless nurture important grass-root creativity.

Even though Björk often refers to Icelandic nature and traditional narratives, she is preoccupied with the concept of difference as defining a structural space rather than a narrative of authenticity. This is an important stance, which helps account for her influence on the borderlines of art and fashion, as distinct from the discourses of national identity successfully explored by many Icelandic fashion designers.

Her extravagant style combines stage costume, global folk and ethno-fashion, girl-in-the-city gear, and fetish wear. It may be argued that all these categories could in fact be put forward as elements of her Icelandic "weirdness," or characteristic of her cosmopolitan hybridity. But it is equally the case that she has used this heterogeneity to refer to the mythic image of Iceland as a space on the border, somewhere between the savage and the civilized. Her international position and status in the world has permitted her to freely transgress or combine cultural boundaries of all types. This is particularly clear in certain of her video representations and in the cover art of her recordings. Many of her costumes look more like wearable art than actual clothing, as her African-Japanese Geisha look, created by Alexander McQueen for the cover art of *Homogenic* (1997). In the music video *Who is it? (Carry My Joy on the Left, Carry My Pain on the Right)* directed by Dawn Shadforth (2004), Björk dances in a silver bell dress accompanied by joker-like bell-clad figures, also designed by Alexander McQueen. The scene is staged on one of the mysterious black sand beaches in southeast Iceland, under the surrealistic brightness of a northern sun, a space of undefined and dreamlike otherness.

While collaborating with some of the most acclaimed designers and artists of the time, Björk also drew attention to several Icelandic artists and designers. They include fashion designers such as Linda Björk Árnadóttir, now head of the Fashion Department at the Iceland Arts Academy, who created dresses for Björk's *Vespertine* tour in 2003.

Another is Hrafnhildur Arnardóttir (b.1969), also known as Shoplifter, who has collaborated with Björk on several occasions, as an artist, stylist, and designer. Most of Arnardóttir's work is inspired from the vanitas symbolism of Victorian flowers, braided with human hair. Her collaboration with Björk and the team of Inez van Lamsweerde and Vinoodh Matadin for the cover art for *Medúlla* (2004) brought the braided hairpieces on the cover of *The New York Times Style Magazine*. The hair sculptures exist in "in this grey area between art, fashion and performance" (Meter 2005), and in 2008 she was commissioned by the Museum of Modern Art in New York to produce a window installation made from colored artificial hair, in collaboration with the artist collective Assume Vivid Astro Focus (a.v.a.f.).

Several other young female artists of the same generation have been working with concepts of domesticity and handicrafts, and used techniques such as traditional needlework, knitting, and crochet in artworks that make reference to issues of gender and sexuality. Hildur Bjarnadóttir (b. 1969) utilizes such grandmotherly domestic practices for works concerned with violence and crime as in her *Shooting Circle*, a round crocheted tablecloth, a white doily, sporting tiny crocheted guns that at first glance could be taken for swans or flowers (Heissler 2005).

The Icelandic Love Corporation, a female art collective formed in 1996 by Sigrún Hrólfsdóttir (b. 1973), Jóní Jónsdóttir (b. 1972), and Eirún Sigurðardóttir (b. 1971), celebrates the feminine as a creative force. They use their crocheted wearable art pieces as costumes in performances in a variety of art contexts such as *Creation—Corruption—Celebration* (2005). The dresses crocheted in natural colors became an inspiration for *The WildWomanWoodooGrannyDoilyCrochet,* one of Björk's most spectacular costumes, commissioned for the cover art of her *Volta* album (2007), according to Icelandic Love Corporation's website, "to make a new character, an electro neon Icelandic domestic joyous force of nature."

By transforming the activity of crocheting into a creative and collective experience, these artists challenge the symbolic Victorian stereotype of a lonely female activity, by making experimental pieces that are not simply garments covering up the body, but more like an independent organic growth, expressing the idea of a feminine sexual vitality. Their art production is characterized by an unusual straightforwardness as a relaxed, cozy practice of friends working together on collective meaningful projects. Assimilating the ephemeral mechanics of fashion, many of their works are created from perishable, fragile materials and come to life while performed in front of an audience. Accordingly, the garments function simultaneously as costumes, fashionable clothing, and wearable art objects. Procedures and material practices such as these provide especially good examples of place-specific preoccupations, crossovers, and hybridity, manifesting the interconnections within contemporary visual culture of the last decade. In this respect, they transcend the boundaries of the art system, referring to other possible frameworks—the fashion show, the circus performance, and the theater of the avant-garde.

## Nature as a Mental Space

Icelandic nature as a subject, as a conceptual idea, and a mental creative space, rather than a geographical fact, was made the subject of work by several Icelandic and international artists during the late 1990s (Sigurjónsdóttir 2006). Since, it has been the theme of several exhibitions such as *Icelandic Fashion and Design—Inspired by Nature*, Cologne 2005 and Berlin 2007, *Dreams of the Sublime and Nowhere in Contemporary Icelandic Art*, Brussels and Reykjavik 2008, and *Volcano Lovers* 2010, Ise Cultural Foundation, New York.

Björk's adaption of the weird or the eccentric in her self-fashioning was rapidly developed and integrated as a part of official branding of "Icelandicness," launched, around the turn of the century, when Reykjavik was selected as European Cultural Capital 2000. The idea of cultural and geographic difference, aided by cultural references inspired by Björk, have since been used in nation branding as has her accompanying emphasis on Iceland's unspoiled nature and her romantic belief in nature's creative force.

However, a romantic striving for communion with nature is far from the concerns of most Icelandic artists, who take their experience of their unspoiled homeland with a grain of salt. In fact, their relationship with the island as a home, geographical site, and mental space is complex and not easily grasped by the foreign observer. Simultaneously, many of these artists are quite aware of the changing role of Iceland in the global ecological and political context. Even as Björk made use of the Icelandic landscape as a stage she also figured Iceland as a *nowhere* as can be seen in her music video *Jóga,* directed by French film director Michel Gondry (1997). More recently she has herself taken a strong political position by launching in 2008 an important ecological conservation project called Náttúra (Nature).

Similarly, Icelandic fashion designers are well aware that they live on the outer limits of Europe. Fashion designer Steinunn Sigurðardóttir is an example of an internationally trained fashion designer who became known through her own collections inspired by Icelandic nature and craft heritage. After studying in Paris and New York, then working with Polo/Ralph Lauren, Calvin Klein, Gucci, and Perla, she created her own label *Steinunn* in 2000. Known first for her knits, she has always been imaginative in her use of texture and structure, exploring the feeling of intimacy and tactility in her designs. She takes inspiration from natural elements such as light, color, and the surfaces of natural forms, and her strongly textured garments are inspired by the organic materiality of Icelandic lava, moss, and black sand. A similar feel for the textures of nature is evident in Björk's description of the music for *Homogenic*, "It should sound like the landscape of Iceland looks ... Like rough volcanoes with soft moss growing over it ... " (Pytlik 2003: 119).

Steinunn is exceptionally focused on craftsmanship, which ensures that her designs are embedded in classical fashion values and *haute couture* traditions, such as cut and style (Figure 2). Her sources are based

**Figure 2**
Steinunn Collection 2007. Costume elements, hoods and bows, as well as the rough texture of Icelandic nature inspire her designs. Photograph: Mary Ellen Mark. Image courtesy of Steinunn.

on traditional domestic production and Icelandic costume elements, incorporating draperies, hoods, and ruffles, although much of the actual production of the garments is based in Italy. Her designs are thus fully integrated within the international fashion system, both through production and diffusion, in contrast to the local grass-root fashion, which has popped up in the wake of the financial crisis, or been fostered by the recent eco-trend, as is the case with designers' collective Vík Prjónsdóttir.

Vík Prjónsdóttir is an example of new ways of conceiving and producing fashion, exploiting the interconnections between global perspectives and local small businesses, an example of the injunction to "think globally and act locally." The collective was created in 2005 by five young Icelandic designers (Brynhildur Pálsdóttir, Egill Kalevi Karlsson, Guðfinna Mjöll Magnúsdóttir, Hrafnkell Birgisson, and Þuríður Rós Sigurþórsdóttir), all of whom have studied and worked abroad. At the time of the collective's formation, the Icelandic wool market had been steadily declining and export of woolen goods had virtually stopped after the collapse of Cold War markets. As a result of this economic shift, only three knitting factories remained in Iceland including Víkurprjón, according to Vík Prjónsdóttir's website. The project thus links ecological principles including sustainability and the use of local resources.

Here too, their designs make reference to the specificity of Iceland's nature, culture, and folklore, manifesting a playful and innovative approach to materials and a relaxed attitude to everyday uses. The result is practical, but at the same time experimental, as can be seen in such nonsense designs as the *Helm of Disguise* (2010), the *Sealpelt* (2005), or the *Beardcap* (2005). The *Snow Blanket* (2010; Figure 3) is aimed at protection in daily life and relates strongly to the notion of domestic warmth.

Even though all their designs are grounded in ancestral sartorial traditions, manifest in forms of helmets, caps, and cloaks, and inspired by folklore rather than material tradition, this design trend is not a nostalgic sublimation of national traditions. Rather than representing a romantic revival, the invocation of survival and protection is self-consciously ironic, linking mythical and heroic narratives to comfort garments and rugs in an entirely contemporary way.

Strong bonds between utility and aesthetics, between tradition and craft, are articulated in the rhetoric of the brand Farmers Market. Bergþóra Guðnadóttir founded the company with her husband, the musician Jóel Pálsson, in 2005. Previously, she had worked for the company 66°North, and still designs some of their most popular outdoor clothing. Under her own brand, Farmers Market, she has revitalized the hand-knit tradition with slimmer, longer profiles and revived the disappearing wool designs from the 1960s and 1970s. As inspiration, she draws upon visual and emotional narratives inspired by her own family album and the "old-fashioned" Cold War wool industry, historically represented by brands like Álafoss and Hilda. She has revived their patterns and brought them back into circula-

**Figure 3**
In Iceland snow is often more dramatic than romantic. *The Snow Blanket* gives warmth and protection from daily life, but it is also a remembrance of all the survivors and those who have passed away. Design by Vík Prjónsdóttir 2010. Photograph: Gulli Már. Image courtesy of Vík Prjónsdóttir.

tion, demonstrating that even things considered as unfashionable and outdated can be a rich resource of memories and emotions for new generations.

As is the case with many young designers, Guðnadóttir was surrounded with domestic creativity during her childhood, where almost everything was made at home. She utilizes photographic snapshots as a trigger for many of her designs and the use of these photographs fosters an atmosphere of authenticity for the brand. Authentic snapshots are mixed with staged fashion shots and simulations of album-type snapshots in a mosaic that creates a nostalgic visual world communicating a feeling of domestic pastness. Using this approach of everydayness as marketing strategy for woolen fashion garments is a novelty in Icelandic design and has also contributed to its popularity with the local tourist market. This is a paradigmatic example of the use of what could be called "identity effects," which can operate successfully in two ways. For young Icelandic consumers, their purchase of the label connotes an identification with a place, a home, a visualized imagined past, while for the foreign consumer, it suggests the possession of something "authentically" Icelandic, an intimate connection, via the act of consumption to another, foreign culture.

## Branding a Small Nation

Nation branding can be a powerful force behind the fashion design of small nations. The branding of Iceland as a product and an export trademark was inaugurated with "Iceland Naturally," a long-term pilot program initiated in 2000 by companies with business interests in the US market (Gudjonsson 2005). The program was meant to represent the "essence" of Iceland, its pristine natural environment, and the creativity of its inhabitants. As "Iceland Naturally" defined it, "As a combined council of Icelandic brands, we take pride in the way our products define Iceland: pure glacial water, clean and renewable energy, sustainable fresh fish, a totally unique travel experience and best of all, our creativity."

Creativity has since been defined in public relations discourse as one of the essential elements of "Icelandicness." An important cultural step, linking tourism with the arts was taken in 2003 when the brand program "Reykjavík Pure Energy" was launched by the city in collaboration with Reykjavik Art Festival and the Iceland Tourist Board. Placing Reykjavik on the map as an exciting contemporary art and fashion city became possible due to the new generation of art, fashion, and design students educated in Berlin, Copenhagen, Milan, Paris, and New York. Since then, Reykjavik has witnessed a substantial growth in art galleries, small designer shops, and boutiques selling fashion and goods made in Iceland.

The city of Reykjavik took a decisive step in promoting fashion by choosing Steinunn as Reykjavik's Artist of the year in 2009. Reykjavik Art Museum opened its doors to fashion shows and organized several exhibitions of design and fashion, including the retrospective of Steinunn fashion in November 2009. The National Museum of Iceland has created a small commercial exhibition space for young and upcoming designers, seeking to encourage a more active interaction between material tradition and contemporary design. New publications of old pattern books and historical research into fashion and cultural traditions are a part of this effort to accelerate and promote various uses of a little-known heritage.

However, the relationship between fashion and nation branding is uneasy, as such branding has strong links to the commercial and marketing identification of country of origin. Iceland is rarely the country of origin for fashion products, since there are so few production units remaining in the country. In a recent interview, when asked about the future of Icelandic fashion in the current period of financial crisis, Steinunn remarked: "We need factories in Iceland to produce real Icelandic fashion. We are producing prototypes, small is beautiful, but not enough to really base something constructive ... Almost all factories were closed 10–15 years ago, but still we have all the craft skills, but they will also be lost if nothing is done. I work with factories in Hong Kong, The Baltic countries, Italy, ... but no factory in Iceland can produce my garments" (Steinunn 2008: 32). Nevertheless, she maintains that her fashion designs are integrally Icelandic, because their aesthetics are derived from the specificities of Icelandic nature (Steinunn 2007: 18).

Iceland was, in fact, one of the earliest victims of the global economic crisis. In the political turmoil and the economic meltdown that followed, the potential of fashion has been identified as an important creative element of survival and recovery. The new Design Centre (Hönnunarmiðstöð Íslands), opened in 2008, defines design and fashion as a valuable national resource, and concludes "it is vital to make use of it."

The crisis seems to have initiated a new kind of inspiration and growth in fashion. As consumer habits were turned upside down, new themes emerged with a concomitant shift in attitudes, lifestyle, marketing, and branding. Many young people lost their jobs, and several have started making fashion for fun, mostly for their friends, starting up new businesses, creating designer nests, pop-up markets, selling through the Internet, and making use of social networks as Flickr and Facebook.

A crisis think-tank and experimental workshops were launched with Björk in collaboration with KLAK (Seed Forum) and the Innovation Centre Iceland (Nýsköpunarmiðstöð Íslands) as creativity had to be sustained. Katrín Júlíusdóttir, then Minister of Industry, Energy, and Tourism, observed in September 2009:

> The creative power of our people is attracting attention and making Iceland a place people want to come and visit ... We must get the message across that we are more than geysers, volcanoes, waterfalls—and now fallen banks. Here you will also find creative people, culture and modern industries. (Júlíusdóttir 2009)

Creativity is here understood as a collective productive process, not ascribed to a particular artistic or individual invention, but rather as a natural sustainable resource. Steinunn has stressed the importance of maintaining skills by reintroducing crafts and home economics into education, not only for fashion and design students, but also for schoolchildren, as was the case in Iceland back in the 1960s and 1970s. She claims that such skills can be the key to sustainable creativity, and facilitates the success of the small, innovative enterprises that have emerged since the economic meltdown in 2008.

## The New Avant-garde

Artists and other agents from the cultural sphere have been active in social and political protests since the meltdown and many believe that Icelandic artists, musicians, and designers have a significant role to play in restoring their country's reputation and economic well-being. "Artists have just kept on doing what they do because they recognize how important our culture is and how extremely necessary it is," says the artist Ragnar Kjartansson, Iceland's Venice Biennale representative in 2009 (Duncan 2009).

New practices and innovative crossovers between design, art, and consumption have emerged. Visual artists, such as Andrea Maack (b. 1977), in collaboration with the new SPARK Design Space, launched her line of scents SMART, CRAFT, and SHARP in the Summer of 2010 in collaboration with French fashion designer Cedric Rivrain and French perfumery producers Apf arômes & parfums.

Maack graduated from the Icelandic Academy of the Arts in 2005. Her work takes as its inspiration the cosmopolitan image of French *haute couture*. Her working method is to translate her pencil and mixed-media drawings into their equivalents as scents. She thus plays with the boundaries between art and consumption, turning the consumption of fashion and scent into an aesthetic experience, which is then recycled into consumption, as her fragrances are now sold as commercial products in designer shops in Reykjavik and Stockholm.

Andrea Maack is an example of the emerging fashion avant-garde, which has taken the decisive step of rejecting all references to the specificities of place. This tendency is represented by a number of young artists and fashion designers such as Bóas Kristjánsson and Mundi Vondi, all of whom work in the non-specific space of contemporary art and fashion. This upcoming generation received their basic training at the Reykjavik Art Academy, where fashion design has been considered a creative, artistic discipline for a decade. Some graduate students have continued their studies in renowned fashion schools abroad and have already attracted attention internationally. Production is small and sales and distribution are mainly through local boutiques and online sales. Some of them profit from their representation in the trendiest boutiques in Paris, London, New York, and Tokyo; others receive commissions for knitwear and leisure wear from locally based companies or new designer shops.

Guðmundur Hallgrímsson (b. 1987), the artist behind the label Mundi Vondi, has already exhibited in elite art fairs such as London's Frieze and the Venice Biennale, while simultaneously collaborating with a Viennese avant-garde group, Gelatin. His art school background is evident in his delight in performance. His designs are a combination of sportswear with traditional suiting, a fun, colorful, mixture of new basic wear and more classical suits. The production is located both in Iceland and in Turkey, but the difficult economic situation in Iceland has made it necessary to bring the production to Iceland, even though it is more expensive to produce in Iceland and the choices of materials and accessories are more restricted. His products are usually sold abroad in cities such as London, Paris, Hong Kong, Barcelona, Amsterdam, and Los Angeles, and more recently, in his newly opened boutique in Reykjavik.

Others, such as Erna Einarsdóttir (b. 1984), have a more classic fashion school background. Erna studied at Gerrit Rietveld Academie, Amsterdam, and Central St Martins, London, and she nurtures a craft-based relationship with her materials, which are mostly fabricated by herself. These are knitted or woven and are mixed with torn nylon hosiery or other "garbage" materials. As she has remarked:

> I don't like going out buying stuff, I find it more fascinating knitting something myself, or if I buy fabric, I work them over, so in the end they don't have anything to do with the look when I bought it. My inspiration can come from art, photography, a state of mind, or from situations around me. The inspiration for my graduate show comes from the riots in Iceland in 2009 ... I have worked much with Icelandic themes, I think that happens often when you don't live any longer in your country, you search for home. (Erna Einarsdóttir, personal communication, December 28, 2009)

A shared goal of most of these new designers is to be truly contemporary, that is by definition edgy, dynamic, and in constant motion. They are creating fashions not based on the traditional forms of production and marketing but rather, on the embrace of eclecticism, borrowing from different sources and combining them with ingenuity and imagination. Until now, these innovative practices have been more visible within the spaces of contemporary art than within the fashion system. These productions, moreover, have been more oriented to the terms of contemporary art than to the terms of the commercial marketplace, belonging to a cutting-edge visual culture, rather than to mass production. New processes of production may well transform this current situation, as signaled in the new production and sales methodologies of artists like Andrea Maack.

Nature versus culture, place-branding versus locally embedded creativity, these are some of the oppositions that structure the Icelandic cultural discourse. The element of costume versus fashion also stands out as an important factor in the work of many Icelandic designers. Could this characteristic be rooted in the simple relationship that Icelandic society has had to clothing, to the traditional ceremonialism growing out of folklore, to the domestic bases of fabrication? Mundi Vondi looks for inspiration in collective grass-root practices and performance. Bóas Kristjánsson points out the absence of real fashion media: "There's a sort of healthy relationship to clothing here, after all we have more of a basic need for warmer clothes and layers. That, and the absence of the fashion media, makes for some interesting outcomes." (*Oyster* 2009)

The current scene is unapologetically local, intuitive, spontaneous, negotiating the new economic realities of scarcity in production instead of abundance. Underpinning these new circumstances is, however, the dream of making it, of being successful, being published and produced in the international media, exhibiting one's creations in Paris or London. The ultimate goal is to be able to sell abroad.

Bóas Kristjánsson says he is not affected by the crisis, as his sales are international. He reveals the fact that the globally extensive fashion business is governed less by purely economic rationales than by networks, contacts, and chance—of being "in the right place at the right time."

## Conclusion

I have argued that the construction of "Icelandicness" in fashion and design is based on the notion of belonging to a particular, specific place, and the affirmation of cultural difference is rooted in domestic, handicraft traditions that are themselves related to climate and geography. These have shaped the branding and marketing of Icelandic products as well as the Icelandic tourist industry.

Art in Iceland, like fashion, does not have an embedded tradition, and the contemporary art has been influenced by the example of the Fluxus movement, which has been an especially significant model within the Art Academy. Interdisciplinary practices, collective work, and diversity of expression have been identified as characteristics of young Icelandic artists; they have been called "hybrid" and considered to be perpetually on the move (Schoen 2007).

Icelandic creativity did not start nor end with Björk, but in retrospect, she is a key figure. Her success as a fashion icon attracted global media attention towards the creative possibilities of a small nation, as she thus encouraged and opened a creative space for others to explore, both artists and designers. Since the late 1990s there has been a tendency to project Björk's own version of an idiosyncratic Icelandicness and grass-root methodology, which was, and still is, so successful in promoting Icelandic music internationally, to the art and fashion scene, and this has been assimilated into arguments for the benefits of nation branding.

Most Icelandic designers still share a strong sense of place and a consciousness of its loss or absence. Such feelings are not connected to the tasks of reconstructing identity or understanding a historical past—not even about confirming the past. Rather, their bonds to place are indicated in the ways they employ visual references (especially photography), indigenous materials, and fabrics associated with warmth and domesticity. This might be translated as a desire to compensate for what has disappeared, as a way of configuring memory, or mediating an imagined past, as analyzed by Jameson:

> If there is any realism left here, it is a "realism" which springs from the shock of grasping that confinement and of realizing that, for whatever peculiar reasons, we seem condemned to seek the historical past through our own pop images and stereotypes about the past, which itself remains forever out of reach. (Jameson 1985: 118)

There seems to be no rule, no overarching structure. The ongoing dynamics are therefore mostly situated outside the fashion system. In this respect, art, music, and fashion are all interrelated in a place, a context, and a set of circumstances that have prompted young people to intensely relate to one another on personal and professional levels.

Most of the new designers operate individually, they are invited into the museum space to exhibit their works, and commercially they have only recently received some support by entities such as the Trade Council of Iceland and the newly created Icelandic Design Centre.

Still, there are some hints as to what the future will be like. Fashion is less dependent on industry, but on creative pools or networks developing out of youth culture, interactive media, and visual education. A relaxed and familiar relationship to fabrics and crafts seem also to be an important element of creative sustainability. However, what the question leaves unanswered is whether fashion designers will survive outside the global fashion system lacking an industry to support them. Whether they will be able to repair, alter, or reinvent a damaged public image of the nation on a long-term level remains an open question. For while fashion is always enchanting, in the Icelandic context it seems to be taking on the more important psychological role of sustaining and re-creating pleasure, desire, and pride within a society marred by identity crises and financial loss.

## References


Brah, Avtar and Annie Coombes (eds). 2000. *Hybridity and Its Discontents*. London: Routledge.

Bourriaud, Nicolas (ed.). 2009. *Altermodern: Tate Triennial*. London: Tate Publishing.

Canclini, Nestor Garcia. 2005. *Hybrid Cultures: Strategies for Entering and Leaving Modernity*. Minneapolis, MN: University of Minnesota.

Duncan, Kevin. 2009. "Ragnar Kjartansson: The Iceland Connection." http://www.banffcentre.ca/about/inspired/2009/summer/articles/iceland.aspx (accessed December 31, 2009).

EFTA. 2009. "History at Glance." http://www.efta.int/about-efta/history.aspx (accessed October 31, 2010).

Ellenberger, Íris. 2008. "Íslendingar í heimi framtíðarinnar: kvikmyndir Vigfúsar Sigurgeirssonar og landkynningarvakningin 1935–40." In Inga Lára Baldvinsdóttir (ed.) *Þjóðin, landið og lýðveldið: Vigfús Sigurgeirsson ljósmyndari og kvikmyndagerðarmaður*, pp. 27–48. Reykjavik: Þjóðminjasafn Íslands.

Ellenberger, Íris. 2009. "Somewhere Between 'Self' and 'Other': Colonialism in Icelandic Historical Research." In Anne Folke Henningsen, Leila Koivunen and Taina Syrjämaa (eds) *Nordic Perspectives on Encountering Foreignness*, pp. 99–114. Turku: University of Turku.

Goodrum, Alison L. 2005. *The National Fabric: Fashion, Britishness, Globalization*. Oxford: Berg.

Gudjonsson, Hlynur. 2005. "Nation Branding." *Place Branding* 1(3): 283–98.

Guðmundsson, Magnús. 1988. *Ull verdur gull, ullariðnaður Íslendinga á síðari hluta 19. aldar og á 20. öld*. Reykjavik: Hið íslenska bókmenntafélag.

Guðmundsson, Sigurður. 1857. "Um kvennbúnínga á Íslandi að fornu og nýju." *Ný Félagsrit* 17: 1–53.

Hálfdanarson, Guðmundur. 2001. *Íslenska Þjóðríkið: Uppruni og endimörk*. Reykjavik: Hið íslenska bókmenntafélag and Reykjavíkur Akademían.

Heissler, Eva. 2005. "Hildur Bjarnadóttir." *List—Icelandic Art News*. http://www.cia.is/news/september05/hildur.htm (accessed November 30, 2009).

Hobsbawm, E. and T. Ranger (eds). 1983. *The Invention of Tradition*. Cambridge: Cambridge University Press.

Jameson, Fredrick. 1985. "Postmodernism and Consumer Society." In Hal Foster (ed.) *Postmodern Culture*, pp. 111–25. London: Pluto Press.

Ingólfsson, Aðalsteinn. 2008. "Andinn, landið og brandið." *Morgunblaðið—Menningarblað/Lesbók* November 22. http://www.mbl.is/mm/gagna safn/grein.html?grein_id=1256444 (accessed December 20 2009).

Júlíusdóttir, Katrín. 2009. "You Are in Control" [speech]. September 23. http://eng.idnadarraduneyti.is/minister/speeches/nr/2766 (accessed December 20, 2009).

Kennedy, Randy. 2006. "The Bjork-Barney Enigma Machine." *The New York Times* April 9. http://www.nytimes.com/2006/04/09/movies/09kenn.html (accessed October 20, 2010).

Meter, William Van. 2005. "Head Case: Meet Björk's Favorite Hair Sculptor." *The New York Times Style Magazine* February 20. http://www.shoplifter.us/index.php?/press/the-new-york-times/ (accessed December 20, 2009).

*Oyster*. 2009. "Iceland Cool—Bóas Kristjánsson." *Oyster* September 17. http://oystermag.com/iceland-cool-boas-kristjansson (accessed December 31, 2009).

Pytlik, Mark. 2003. *Björk: Wow and Flutter.* Toronto: ECW

*Rokk í Reykjavík*. 1982. *Film*. Dir. Friðriksson, Friðrik Þór. Sena DVD, 2008.

Schoen, Christian. 2007. "Observation from Inside and Out." *LIST—Icelandic Art News* Summer: 4–7.

Sigurðsson, Helgi Snær. 2009. "Manstu eftir ... Don Cano?" *Morgunblaðið* 9. http://www.mbl.is/mm/gagnasafn/grein.html (accessed November 30, 2009).

Sigurjónsdóttir, Æsa. 2006. "A Strange Place Called Nowhere" In Jonathan Clarkson and S. O'Reilly (eds) *Sense in Place*, pp. 209–13. Cardiff: University of Wales.

Sigurjónsdóttir, Æsa. 2008. *Til gagns og til fegurðar. Sjálfsmyndir í ljósmyndum og klæðnaði 1860–1960*. Reykjavik: National Museum.

Steinunn, 2007. "Undir áhrifum himins og hafs." *Fréttablaðið* August 12: 18.

Steinunn. 2008. "Vantar verksmiðjur á Íslandi." *Fréttablaðið* December 20: 32.

Volk, Gregory. 2000. "Art on Ice—Icelandic Art." *Art in America* September: 40–5.

*Fashion Theory,* Volume 15, Issue 2, pp. 259–266
DOI: 10.2752/175174111X12954359478843
Reprints available directly from the Publishers.
Photocopying permitted by licence only.


# The Prospects and Perils of Creating a Viable Fashion Identity

**Norma M. Rantisi**

Norma M. Rantisi is Associate Professor in the Department of Geography, Planning & Environment at Concordia University, Montreal, Canada. Her research interests are centered on local economic development in cities, with a focus on the social and spatial organization of cultural industries. Her recent publications examine restructuring in the Montreal apparel industry and government policies to promote design innovation.
norma.rantisi@gmail.com

## Abstract

In a context of deindustrialization, both firms and local governments within "second-tier" fashion centers are striving to develop a distinct identity from which to market products and place. For cultural industries such as a fashion, this endeavor requires a set of localized capabilities. In particular, a network of relations between interdependent, industry actors is critical for cultivating a common culture and shared artistic sensibilities. This article considers the role that two intermediary institutions—the independent boutique and the fashion show—can play in promoting localized linkages and aesthetics.

**KEYWORDS: fashion design, identity, second-tier cities, deindustrialization, fashion week**

## A New Century and New Opportunities for Fashion

One of the key features marking the economic landscape of advanced capitalist societies at the turn of the twenty-first century is the decline of manufacturing and the rise of an economy centered on knowledge and innovation. Whereas previously, competitiveness was defined in terms of the access to inputs for large-scale production—raw materials, land, labor, and infrastructure—today globalization and the rise of new technologies have altered (and in many cases, leveled) the economic playing field. Access to inputs has become ubiquitous, and competitiveness is now recast in terms of an ability to adapt readily to shifting, global trends through a more creative use of inputs. Within this new economic paradigm, emphasis is placed on aesthetic innovation and the production of signs and symbols to distinguish products as well as places in the international marketplace (Lash and Urry 1994).

The focus on aesthetic innovation in today's economy presents both challenges and opportunities for industries such as fashion, especially for those situated in places defined as "second-tier" within the international fashion pyramid. On the one hand, this new paradigm implies a shift in economic organization and strategy on the part of apparel firms, many of which are now outsourcing assembly to low-wage contexts and focusing on design, marketing and service-oriented activities. In pursuing this strategy, however, firms within the "second-tier," or what Larner *et al.* (2007) have termed "not-so-global" centers, face a challenge in that their symbolic capital is often limited. In contrast to the so-called "first-tier" centers, "second-tier" centers rarely have the same cultural resources (e.g. prominent museums and design exhibitions) or established design traditions, not to mention commercial resources from which firms can benefit (Gilbert 2006; Larner *et al.* 2007). On the other hand, as several of the articles in this special issue illustrate, the new economic paradigm also implies that fashion has become a target of government policy. Economic development officials are now keen to promote cultural industries as a means to mark their locales as innovative places in which to work, live, play or invest, and fashion in particular is deemed to epitomize novelty. From the perspective of policymakers, fashion contributes to place-branding and the promotion of tourism; it also contributes to defining the aesthetics of a place which in turn, can shape the design and marketing of cultural products. Scholars such as geographer Allen Scott (2000) and sociologist Harvey Molotch (1996) contend that the relationship between cultural products and place is a symbiotic one from which a distinct identity can emerge (e.g. Hollywood or Broadway). The key challenge is in identifying the attributes that can nurture a symbiotic relation, and in channeling government support towards the development of a distinct yet *viable* fashion identity.

## What Constitutes a Distinct Fashion Identity?

Since fashion, by definition, defies one "look," one could argue that the identity of a fashion center is constituted not by a particular national style or regional costume, but by the localized capabilities that produce new styles or redefine old ones. Such capabilities include the presence of key industry activities—production, design, marketing and distribution; what is more important, however, is the interaction and coordination between industry actors. This is particularly significant for adapting in a context of globalization, characterized by heightened competition and the constant flow of information. A network of relations can help to filter and circulate the most useful information; it can also facilitate knowledge creation and learning i.e., the process of creating new designs by altering or combining existing information. Moreover, apart from anchoring external flows of information and best practices, a network of relations between local, interdependent actors can facilitate the development of trust and shared business conventions. These social ties, in turn, make it easier for firms to identify new sources of inspiration and support. Thus, the "network" can enable fashion actors to stay attuned to the prevailing design and consumption imperatives of a symbolic economy as well as to access the resources and networks needed to respond to these imperatives.

Due to the economic trends cited above, researchers are now actively seeking the ingredients for building up a set of localized capabilities. Allen Scott, for example, in writing about the challenges faced by the Los Angeles industry, cites the need for the following elements: training and research institutes that can supply new sources of labor and technology; a cluster of skilled and specialized subcontractors; a promotional infrastructure (fashion shows, events, media); links between fashion and other cultural industries; and more generally, an evolving design tradition that incorporates place-specific elements (2002: 1304). His emphasis is clearly on the production, design and marketing dimensions of the industry. Those dimensions are central to the constitution of an autonomous fashion industry, as is evident in the case studies presented here. However, there are two key elements that are overlooked in Scott's analysis. First, as Gilbert (2006) observes, consumption is not accorded a place in his recommendations, and yet today fashion centers are as much shopping meccas as they are production or design hubs. Second, and important for the discussion here, Scott emphasizes the need for links between fashion and other cultural industries, but neglects to specify the need for links *within* the fashion industry in his policy prescriptions. As Skov notes in her article (this issue), different industry actors often have divergent interests; thus, stronger ties are essential for identifying potential points of convergence or for establishing new bases for partnerships. In the sections that follow, I provide examples of two intermediary institutions that can forge linkages and promote a set of place-based aesthetics: the independent boutique and the fashion show.

## The Role of Boutiques in Producing Fashion as Industry and Place

Boutiques are important intermediaries within the industry, particularly for emerging centers that are trying to build up an identity. Firstly, retail distribution channels in general are key conduits of information on consumer preferences. In the case of the large retail chains, this information is often mediated by a fashion buyer and based on quantitative data (e.g. data on which products are selling). Smaller retail formats, such as independent boutiques, however, allow for closer and more frequent exchanges with the buyer, who is most often the boutique owner. And since independent boutique owners often communicate with customers in their shop, the feedback they supply to a fashion designer is of a qualitative nature, relating to specific design elements, and can help the designers become better attuned to local sensibilities (see Entwistle 2006).

The advantages that boutiques confer are even greater in the case when the fashion designer is the owner. A number of the articles in this issue highlight the importance of the boutique for a fashion designer's career. The opening of their own boutique plays a role in building up the designer's status and visibility in the fashion marketplace (see de Cléir, this issue; Soares, this issue). In my own research on the Montreal fashion industry, designers indicated that part of the appeal of having their own boutique was having complete control over how their products were presented and the kind of information conveyed to the customer. In addition, they could acquire direct feedback from the customer, so the relationship was unmediated.

The qualitative relations built up through the boutique serve as a means for the designer or fashion firm to enhance their retail experience and acquire tailored knowledge. These ties also benefit the fashion industry as a whole. As mentioned above, the exchange of information between industry actors (in this case, consumers, retailers and designers/producers) is critical for developing shared business conventions and perspectives. Moreover, boutiques add character to a retail landscape increasingly overrun by international chains and big-box stores. The distinctiveness of the boutique in terms of interior design, architecture, product offering, as well as buyer–supplier relations contributes to the broader fashion aesthetic of a place. In her article, de Cléir suggests that a smaller fashion center has the advantage in that it can offer a "boutique" or individual experience, as compared with the established centers; a diversified retail landscape—particularly the presence of independent boutiques—contributes to that experience.

## The Role of Fashion Weeks in Producing Fashion as Industry and Place

Fashion Weeks are another intermediary institution that can promote relations among actors within the fashion industry and aid in the construction of a fashion identity. It is not coincidental that many emerging centers, e.g. Amsterdam, Berlin, Cork and Oslo, have established their own fashion weeks within the last six years. These shows are deemed critical for promoting local design talent to buyers and to the fashion media. As a form of entertainment, they can also generate interest and engagement on the part of consumers (see Skov *et al.* 2009). Beyond these functions, however, the shows can also provide a space in which ideas are circulated and connections are forged. The Portugal Fashion Week, discussed in Soares' article, is a case in point. The event seeks to showcase Portuguese design talent but also to establish partnerships between designers and apparel firms.

Another example that illustrates the potential for the fashion show to function as an intermediary is Montreal Fashion Week (MFW). The organizers use MFW to promote partnerships by integrating a number of initiatives as part of the program. First, the program includes encounters, such as breakfast meetings, where designers can network with the press, buyers and other designers in a less formal or structured setting. Second, there is an initiative called Le Showroom, where booths are set up and local designers can exhibit samples of their collection to visiting buyers. This initiative not only links designers to buyers but also provides a space for observation and exchange, with the potential to link designers to other designers or to local manufacturers. Third, the event organizers survey a select number of foreign buyers and journalists, and ask them for qualitative feedback about what they liked or did not like about the products they saw. The feedback is then passed on to producers (personal interviews with one of the event organizers and fashion designers 2007–8). Finally, the MFW program includes other activities, such as concerts, theater plays and a visit to the Cirque du Soleil costume studio, to forge linkages between fashion and other related industries and to capitalize on the cachet of Montreal's other cultural products (see Sigurjónsdóttir, this issue; Weller 2008).

By providing spaces, activities and events that facilitate the coming together of industry actors, shows such as MFW offer designers the opportunity to communicate their products in more dynamic and active forms, not just through passive presentation (see also Soares' discussion of Ana Salazar's shows, this issue). Moreover, this has implications for how they are integrated into global (i.e. "first-tier") networks of buyers and fashion media. Rather than merely reproducing the existing fashion hierarchy, designers can influence the terms by which they engage other actors.

## Realizing New Fashion Dreams—The Way Forward?

The examples above illustrate a role for intermediaries in fostering the place-based relations and aesthetics that can distinguish an emerging center.[1] Given the tie-in that fashion has to other cultural products and its economic multiplier effects (e.g. fashion magazines, fashion photography, advertising, modeling, and other related activities), government support in this process is warranted. Yet to date, this is where a major challenge lies. As mentioned in several articles (Melchior, Sigurjónsdóttir, Skov, this issue; see also Gilbert 2006), there is a tendency for governments to adopt a top-down, instrumental and outward-focused policy orientation, since fashion is viewed primarily as a medium for place marketing rather than place making. This translates into a limited vision of what constitutes a fashion identity and an emphasis on branding initiatives, e.g. the fashion show as a stage rather than genuine intermediary. Moreover, the depiction of fashion centers in relative terms, i.e. how they compare with long-standing centers such as Paris or New York, places unrealistic expectations on these centers and reinforces a perception that they are operating on the margins. Thus, even as the contemporary preoccupation with novelty offers up possibilities for new fashion dreams and for reimagining centers as distinctive rather than marginal, current policy approaches preclude the investment in resources and time needed to develop a localized design tradition, such as support for designer–investor and designer–buyer linkages (see Teunissen, this issue). The transformation of a dream into reality requires a new mindset and more inclusive, bottom-up policies that can solidify place-based competencies towards the development of a viable fashion identity.

## Note

1. The examples are illustrative but by no means exhaustive. As Teunissen's article (this issue) reminds us, Belgium, home to the "Antwerp Six," does not have an official fashion week. However, the country is home to the Flanders Fashion Institute, which serves as intermediary institution to support designers in their business endeavors and showcase their products.

## References

Entwistle, J. 2006. "The Cultural Economy of Fashion Buying." *Current Sociology* 54(5): 704–24.

Gilbert, D. 2006. "From Paris to Shanghai: The Changing Geographies of Fashion's World Cities." In C. Breward and D. Gilbert (eds) *Fashion's World Cities*, pp. 3–32. Oxford: Berg.

Larner, W., M. Molloy and A. Goodrum. 2007. "Globalization, Cultural Economy, and Not-So-Global Cities: The New Zealand Designer Fashion Industry." *Environment and Planning D: Society and Space* 25(3): 381–400.

Lash, S. and J. Urry. 1994. *Economies of Signs and Space*. London: Sage.

Molotch, H. 1996. "LA as Product: How Design Works in a Regional Economy." In A.J. Scott and E.W. Soja (eds) *The City: Los Angeles and Urban Theory at the End of the Twentieth Century*, pp. 225–75. Berkeley, CA: University of California Press.

Rantisi, N.M. 2009. "Cultural Intermediaries and the Geography of Designs in the Montréal Fashion Industry." In G. Rusten and J.R. Bryson (eds) *Industrial Design and Competitiveness: Spatial and Organization Dimensions*, pp. 93–116. Basingstoke: Palgrave Macmillan.

Scott, A.J. 2000. *The Cultural Economy of Cities*. London: Sage.

Scott, A.J. 2002. "Competitive Dynamics of Southern California's Clothing Industry: The Widening Global Connection and its Local Ramifications." *Urban Studies* 39(8): 1287–306.

Skov, L., E. Skjold, F. Larsen, B. Moeran and F.F. Csaba. 2009. *The Fashion Show as an Art Form*. *©reative Encounters* Working Paper. Copenhagen: Copenhagen Business School.

Weller, S. 2008. "Beyond Global Production Networks: Australian Fashion Week's Trans-sectoral Synergies." *Growth and Change* 39(1): 104–122A.

*Fashion Theory,* Volume 15, Issue 2, pp. 267–272
DOI: 10.2752/175174111X12954359478889
Reprints available directly from the Publishers.
Photocopying permitted by licence only.


# National Identities and International Recognition

**Simona Segre Reinach**

Simona Segre Reinach is a Cultural Anthropologist teaching at IULM University in Milan and Iuav University in Venice as a Contract Professor. She is currently undertaking research in China in a collaborative project on Sino-Italian joint ventures in the textile and fashion industry. She has written three books in Italian and several articles and essays in English.
simona.segre@gmail.com

**Abstract**

The intensification of production relocation has changed the geography of fashion and the relations between "made in" and national creativity. The possibility of creating fashion, i.e. of being recognized as "author countries," is part of a process in which hierarchies and roles are being constantly renegotiated according to the contexts and players concerned.

KEYWORDS: fashion design, identity, globalization, nation, city

More than anything else, my research into Sino-Italian joint ventures, i.e. the ways in which Chinese and Italians transform garments and accessories into fashionable objects, has helped me to understand the extent to which fashion identities are increasingly relational, interdependent, and constantly fluctuating between self-perception and external recognition. On the often stereotyped ideas and prejudices—and not only on the capacity to manufacture something that is aesthetically relevant—depends the reputation of a city, a nation or a culture to claim a role in the global fashion system. The autarchic experiment of Italian fashion during the Fascist period, for example, shows that, while at the time an Italian fashion did exist with many premises for what was going to become "made in Italy" fashion, the fact that it was limited to the Italian context prevented its very existence. In the 1950s it was the USA that "created" an Italian fashion, recognizing it as such in comparison with the Parisian one. It is well-known that until the mid-twentieth century in Europe, the USA, and in countries colonially linked to the West, fashion mainly arose as an "emancipation" from Paris. French fashion, with the production and cultural system of Parisian *haute couture* and the couturiers, was affirmed as a benchmark for any other fashion attempting to emerge. The *American Beauty* exhibition (FIT Fashion Institute of Technology, New York, November–December 2009) investigated the roots of American fashion since its "liberation" from French hegemony in the period after the Second World War. Many fashion designers were directly defined in relation to what was coming from France, like Claire McCardell considered "the gal who defied *Dior*," according to the Maryland Women's Hall of Fame Online. Until the mid-1950s, many fashion nations or cities alternated the imitation of Parisian models with their inevitable adaptation to local tastes and culture, in view of a more or less imminent emancipation from Paris (Steele 1988). In the 1930s Shanghai was considered the "Paris of the East," where to Parisian domination was added the colonial one. Since the 1980s the process seems to have been completed. A huge increase in fashion cities, as Lise Skov (this issue) points out, characterizes the contemporary scenario. In our era of globalization, fashions are springing up all over the place, as is demonstrated by the increasingly numerous fashion weeks taking place in the furthest-flung "fashion cities" (Ling 2006). The articles in this issue do, however, suggest some important corrections. I will concentrate on two correlated, but distinct, aspects. The first is that there was no single emancipation process from Paris, or rather the initial movement to equal Paris included different forms of emancipation. As clearly emerges from the articles in this issue, under the label of "national fashion," different anthropologies of production and consumption develop, which tie in with the local sartorial histories of each nation or city. As Teunissen says (personal communication, New European Fashion Centres Conference, Copenhagen Business School, January 20–1, 2010), "clearly the different European countries have a different taste in fashion or style, as well as a different attitude to clothes and fashion. The question is whether this is also based on a different design process." There have been many different ways to achieve or attempt to achieve a "dream" of fashion, as is clear in the cases examined here: Portugal, Denmark, Sweden, Norway, Iceland, Holland, Belgium, and Ireland. One indicator is linked to the vicissitudes of outsourcing. The intensification of production relocation has in fact changed not only the geography of fashion, but also the relations between "made in" and national creativity. In some cases it has made sartorial identities more fragile; in others it has strengthened them, granting greater freedoms of expression. For countries where the production tradition of textiles is prevalent, such as Ireland, "with great skills of carding, spinning and warping woolen yarn," says Síle de Cléir (personal communication, New European Fashion Centres Conference, Copenhagen Business School, January 20–1, 2010), the loss of the manufacturing side has left the country, so to speak, a "fashion orphan." For the local Irish boutiques attempting to put forward innovative forms of consumption, it is important not to oppose global and local, center and periphery, but to start a process to match the global context with the local identities. Iceland, on the contrary, may relaunch a postmodern identity linking fashion and art, presenting it as a mix between uncontaminated nature and multimediality, without attempting to manage local manufacture, which that has never been very significant. As Æsa Sigurjónsdóttir writes (personal communication, New European Fashion Centres Conference, Copenhagen Business School, January 20–1, 2010) on Iceland, "it is a fashion that is not based on production and marketing but on creativity and flux." The model here is of course Björk. The case of Belgium, put forward by Teunissen, shows instead that its having been to a certain extent a producer for France, its domineering neighbor, has marked its creative destiny in a very different way from that of Holland. While Belgium has operated mainly in the shadow of Paris, developing excellent techniques and craftsmanship, but in a less articulate and in many ways less clear aesthetic identity, Holland has presented itself with a specific aptitude. Dutch fashion has always reflected its egalitarian ideology, expressed in a style marked by sobriety, then becoming modernist, which is still visible today, Teunissen writes, even in the most eccentric Dutch fashion designers such as Viktor & Rolf; as if the failure of "emancipation" had also led to Belgian fashion's weaker identity compared with Dutch fashion which, since 1700, had set out to be an alternative to France.

In the present-day "catwalk economy," a concept expressed by Löfgren and Willim (2005) to which Marie Riegels Melchior refers in her article (this issue), in order to be successful as a fashion nation, it may not be necessary to have had a manufacturing past but it is, however, necessary to achieve international recognition. The role of governments is much more significant than it used to be. And here I come to the second point mentioned above, the growing importance for the national identity of being able to offer an internationally recognized fashion profile. Each nation has a vested interest in being recognized as a place of creativity and aesthetics. We might call this a "dressed power," as a consequence of the catwalk economy. Fashion itself is no longer an issue regarding ways in which people dress up and ways in which brands are distributed, but the chance for countries to take part in the global exchange, the interconnections marking our period. Fashion is not just making clothes, but also an attribute that nations no longer seem to be able to do without.

For a country or a city, expressing an immediately recognizable aesthetic has become an important corollary to communicate political and economic strength. Much more than in the past, fashion has not only the task to reflect and represent social or individual needs, but has equipped itself with the chance to construct *ex novo* territories in which the imaginary is creatively set free. This is because, as Diane Crane explains, "unlike most of the types of production and commercial activities, fashion expresses a very elaborate culture, composed of symbols, ideologies and lifestyles" (2010: 113) to draw on. Apart from the differences in origins and current development, all the articles in this special issue point out the broadening of the range of fashion. From a product that has to demonstrate its equal seductive capacity to "Parisian fashion," it has become a concept used to express the importance, and symbolic and cultural capital of a country. Fashion is used by governments to promote tourism, to weave celebratory and competitive relationships in a sort of contemporary *potlatch* in which the objects traded are garments, designers, and images in the media. This is why, despite globalization, or perhaps because of it, local fashion cultures and national fashions are developing together with international exchanges. Its distinctiveness from the romantic nationalism of the past, Marie Riegels Melchior explains, lies in the relational nature of the game, in its fluctuating, and being only apparently linked to geographical boundaries. Since the 1980s fashion has become a widespread tool for communication that contributes to defining the panorama of globalized popular culture.

The picture has become broader and far reaching, as is shown in the various statements by governors, mayors, and politicians wishing to ensure for their city or nation the "fifth," "sixth" or "seventh" place after Paris, New York, London, Milan and, depending on the charts, Tokyo and Shanghai. In reality Paris, together with New York and followed by London and Milan, is still the most important hub where designers or brands have to make their name, according to the study carried out by Godart (2009), in order to earn international success, just as happened for Yohji Yamamoto, Issey Miyake, and Rei Kawakubo in the 1980s. But if we consider fashion not only as a system of companies–designers–consumers, but also analyze its growing role as an "ambassador" of a country, then the race for the fifth or sixth place sought after by so many countries and cities is not so strange. In an interview for an Italian daily, the Chinese fashion designer Guo Pei declared that the Chinese government has at last understood that fashion changes one's image in the world. The China guiding the world economy naturally also needs aesthetic recognition, so far obscured by the prevalent vision of the country as the "factory of the world" (Finnane 2008). This is also true for the various European countries and cities that have until now been peripheral compared with Paris, New York, London, and Milan, such as Copenhagen, Stockholm, Helsinki, Dublin, Reykjavik, and Porto. The "fashion dream of small nations" is the result of a polycentric system and an impellent need to overturn the old nineteenth-century ranking of cities (Gilbert and Breward 2006). At the same time it goes further than that. The drive for national identification or rather for national ways of making fashion is much more pervasive and general. Governments, as the articles presented here point out, support fashion as an economic and political necessity. The "production" of fashion in the broadest sense, as more complex than just manufacturing, is necessary as a prerequisite for an active participation in the culture of globalization. Establishing a "recognized" fashion goes way beyond the original meaning of succeeding in matching a more or less specialized textile and garment production with an-up-to date aesthetics. The fashion nation might require actions of communication to adjust old stereotypes to global interactions. "Nordic fashion," for example, is a concept that has taken the place of the mainly functionalistic interpretation of "Scandinavian design." The Scandinavian countries to which postwar Europe attributed the invention of functional design must take another road leading them towards the recognition of fashion, as Marie Riegels Melchior writes. Fresh imaginaries must be evoked, transforming Scandinavian countries "from design nations to fashion nations," in the same way as notions of "Asian look" or "Asian fashion" are preferable to "Oriental fashion" for recent scholars in the field of Asian fashion. German fashion is another interesting example: almost clashing with the traditional image of the country, it thus becomes "cool" when associated with Berlin, the capital of digital fashion. The construction process of fashion nations is very advanced and involves many other sectors besides fashion. Because it is concrete, but at the same time also the most immaterial of products, fashion lends itself to being an optimal synthetic indicator of a nation's position, amidst memory, mystification, and imaginary.

## References


Crane, D. 2010. *L'industria della moda e la globalizzazione della cultura* in *Geografie della moda*. Emanuela Mora (ed.). Milan: Franco Angeli.

Finnane, A. 2008. *Changing Clothes in China*. New York: Columbia University Press.

Gilbert, D. and C. Breward (eds). 2006. *Fashion's World Cities*. Oxford: Berg.

Godart, F. 2009. *Paris est-elle toujours la capitale de la mode? Identité et positionnement des espaces urbains dans le réseau global de la mode in Paris métropole dans le monde*. Paris: Fréderic Gilli.

Ling, W. (ed.). 2006. *Game on: The World Fashion Conquest* [exhibition catalog]. London: Exhibit.

Löfgren, O. and R. Willim. 2005. *Magic Culture and the New Economy*. Oxford: Berg.

Steele, V. 1988. *Paris Fashion: A Cultural History*. Oxford: Berg.